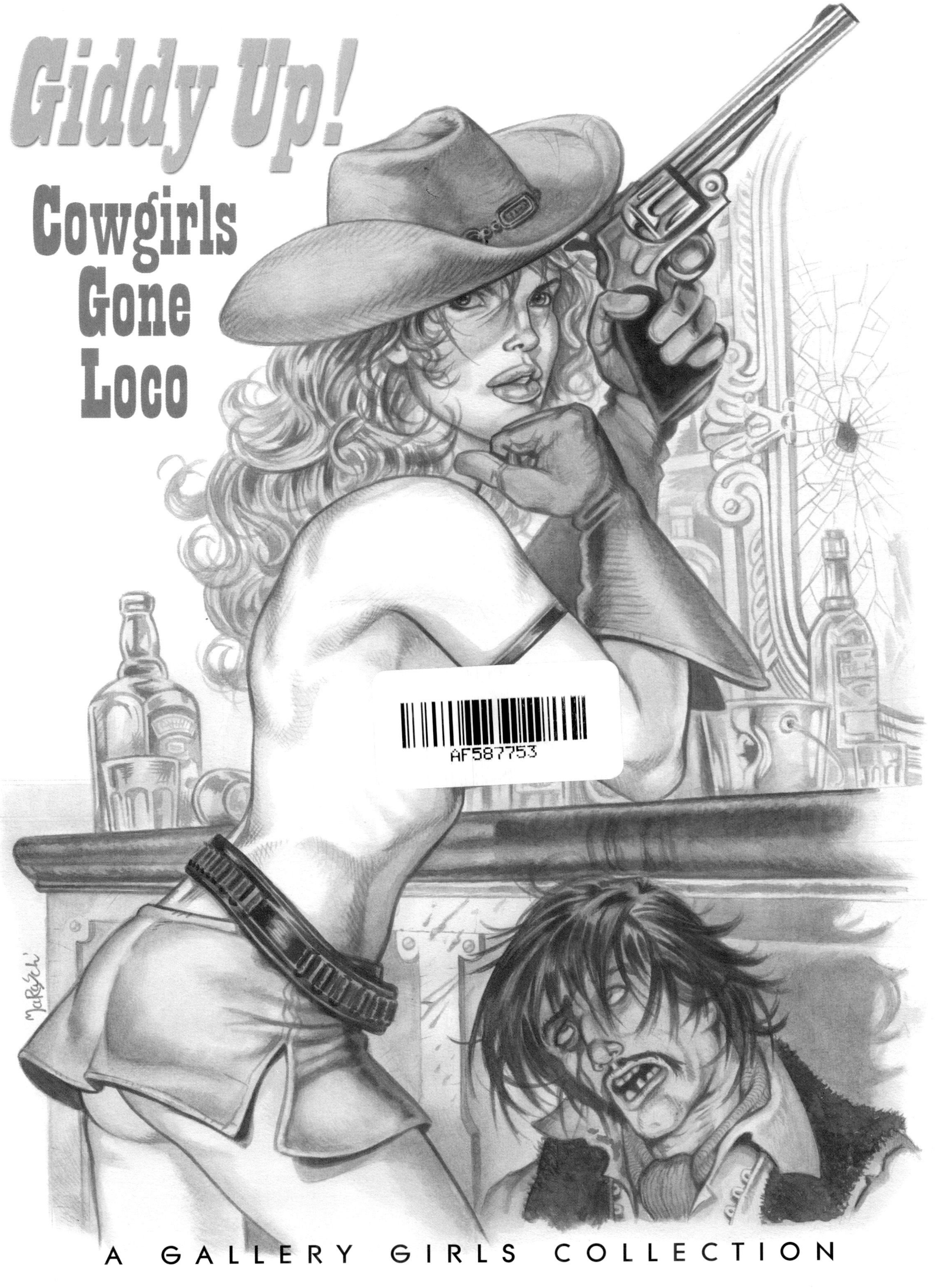
Giddy Up!
Cowgirls
Gone
Loco
A GALLERY GIRLS COLLECTION

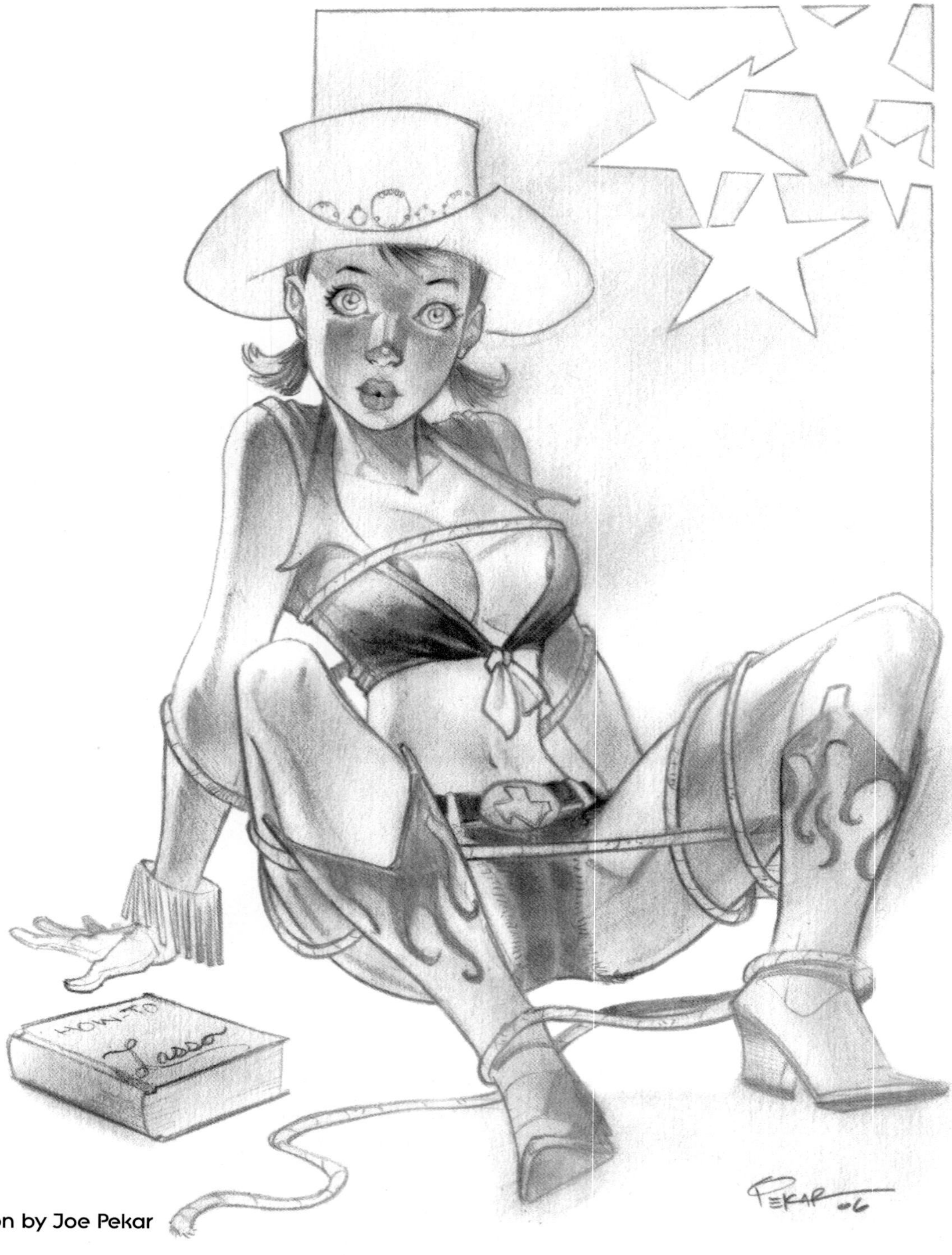

Illustration by Joe Pekar

GIDDY UP!

Volume One

Book design by Grassy Knoll Studios.

Published by
SQP Inc.
PO Box 248 - Columbus, NJ 08022

Sal Quartuccio & Bob Keenan - Publishers

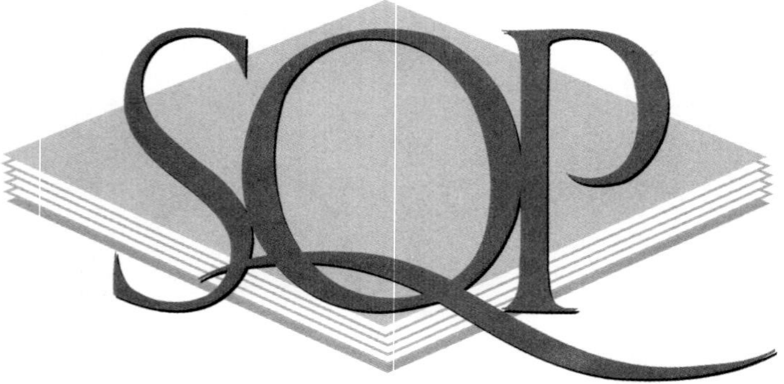

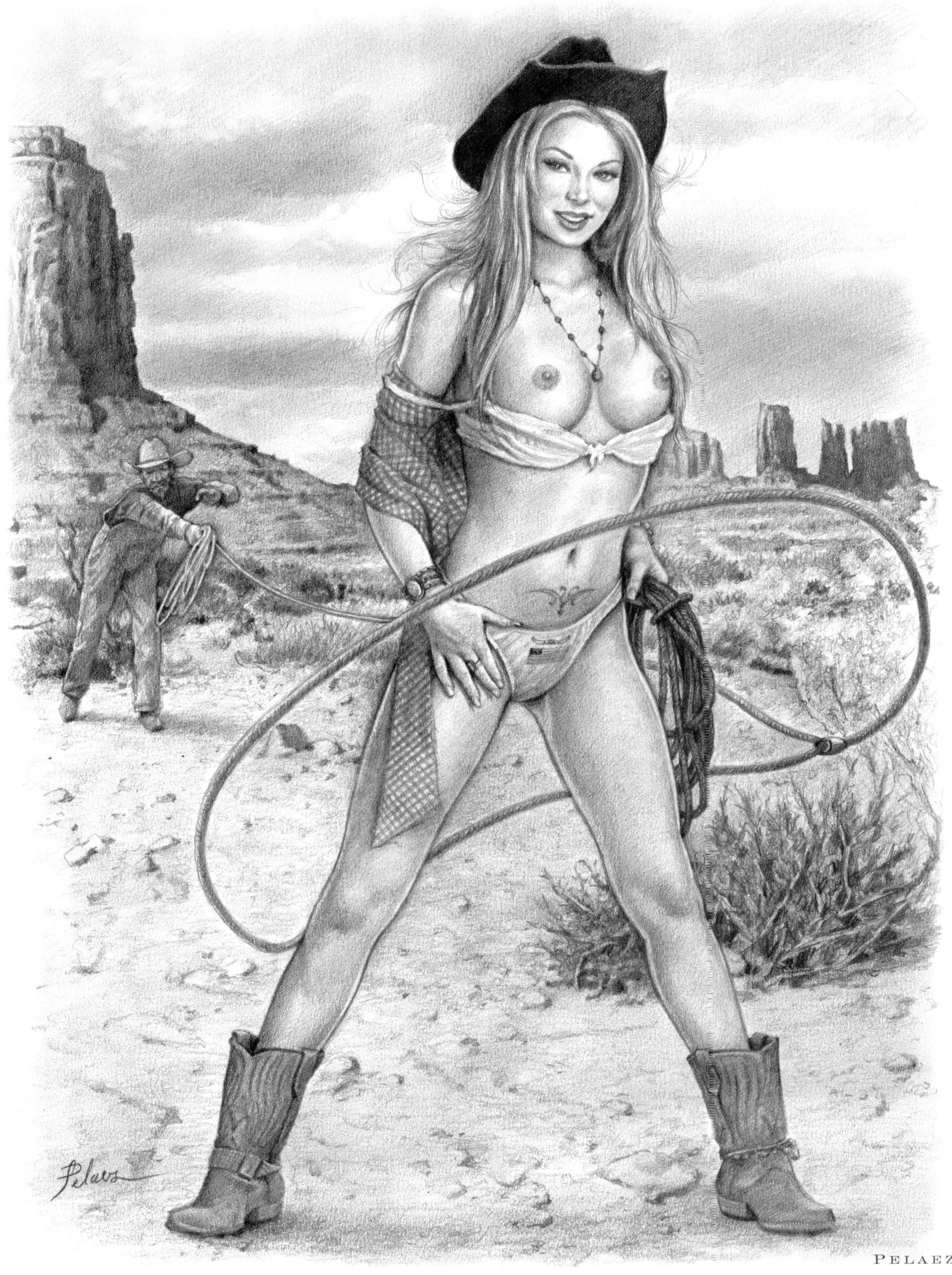

PELAEZ

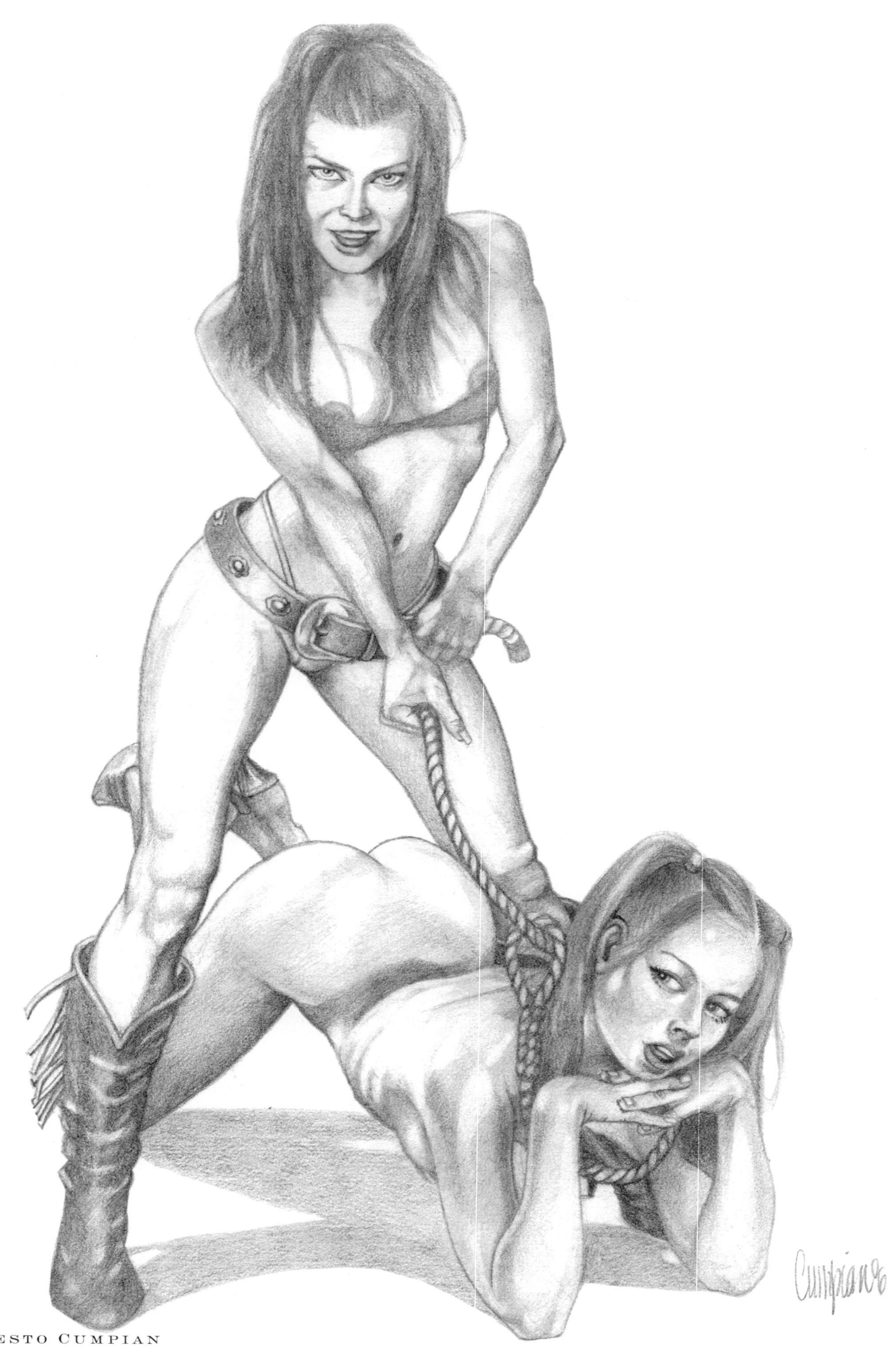

Ernesto Cumpian

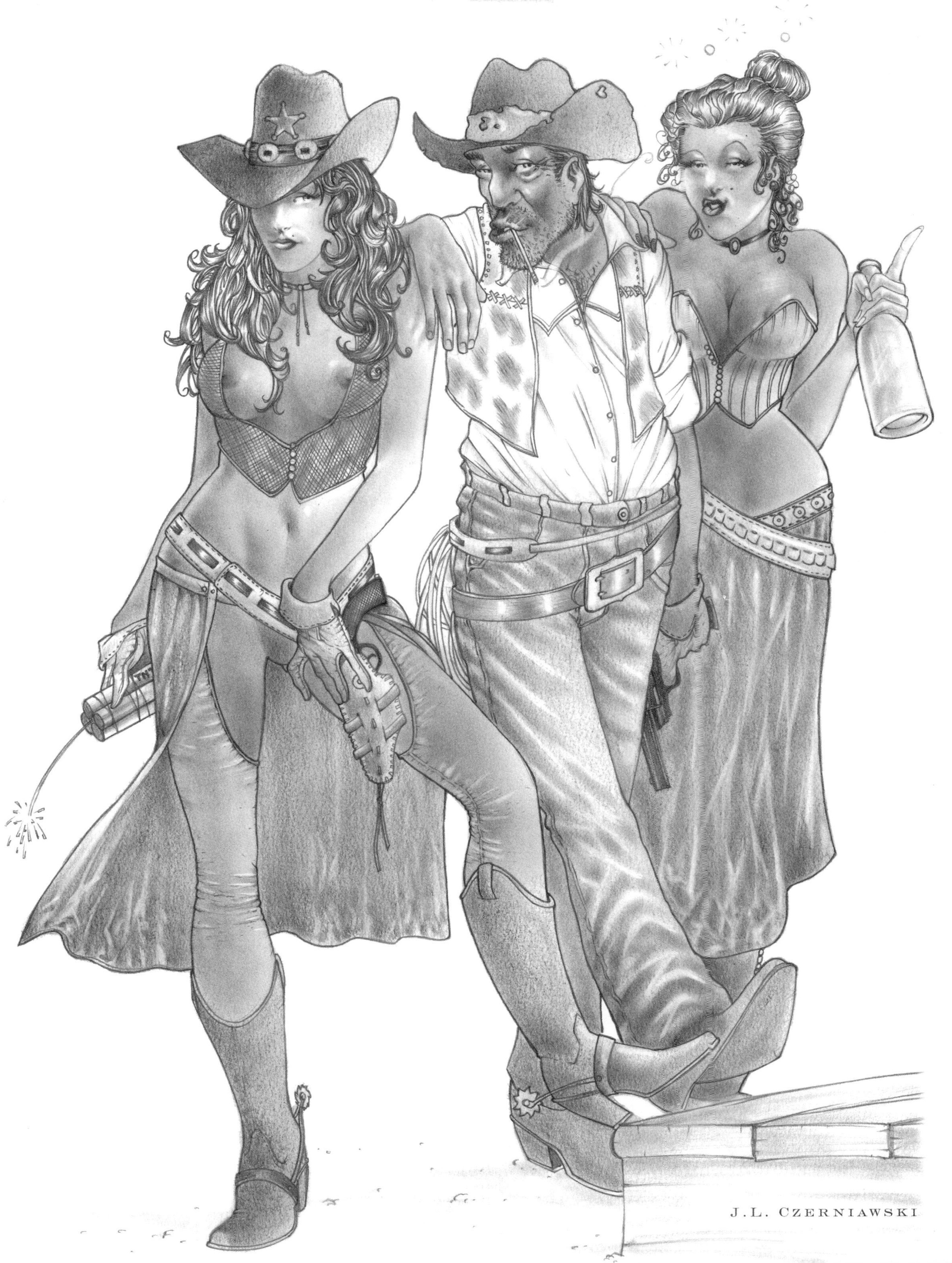
J.L. Czerniawski

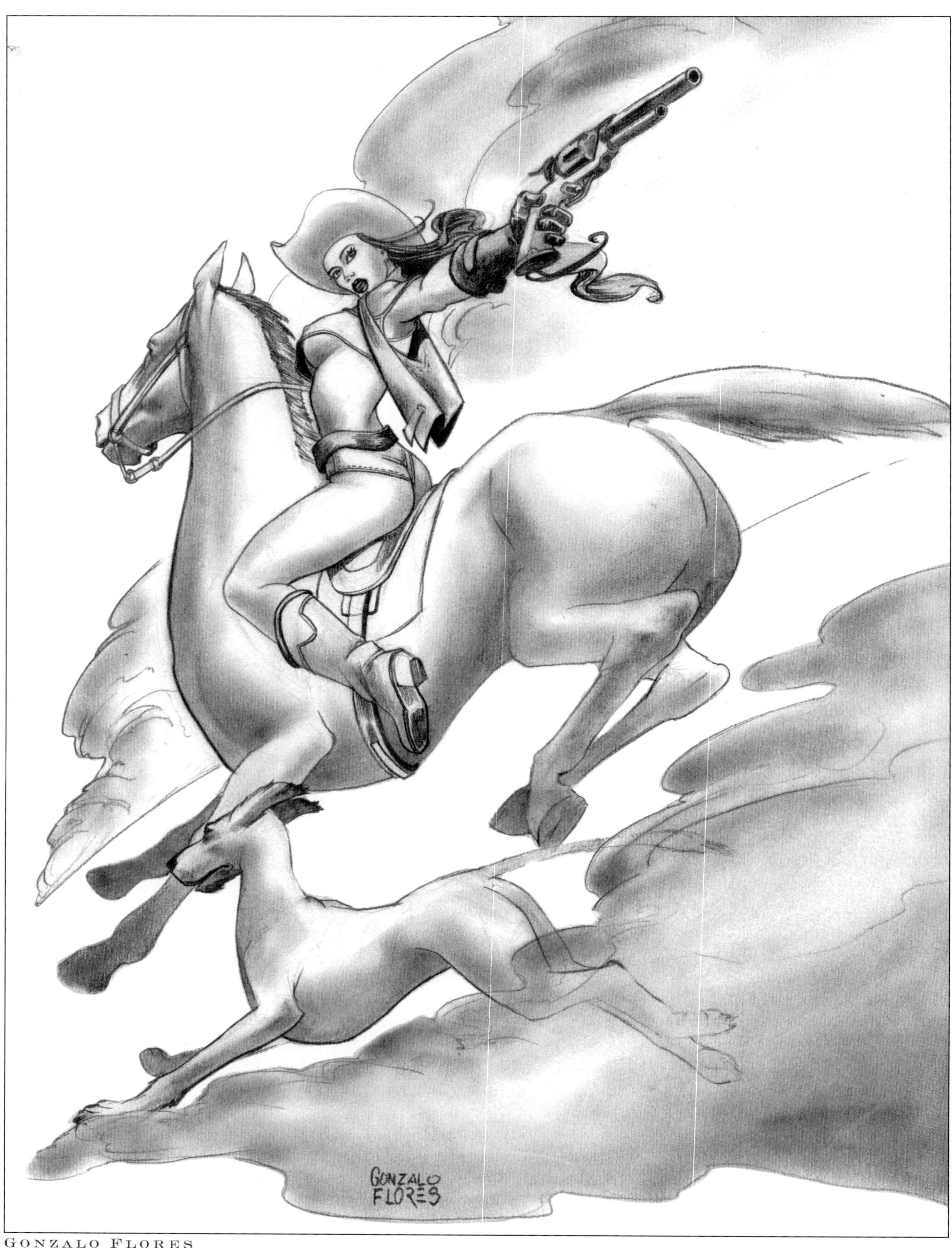

Gonzalo Flores

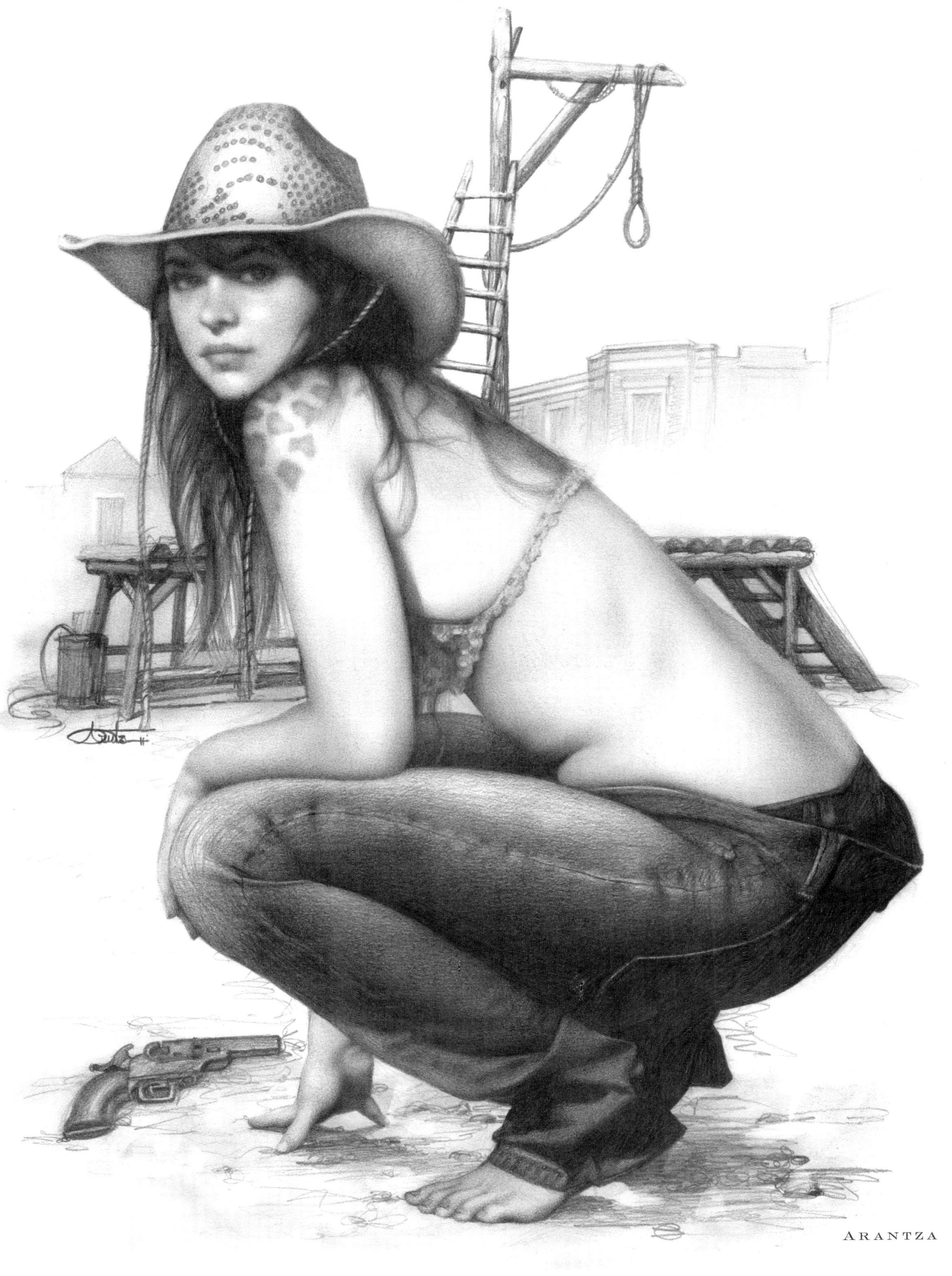

Arantza

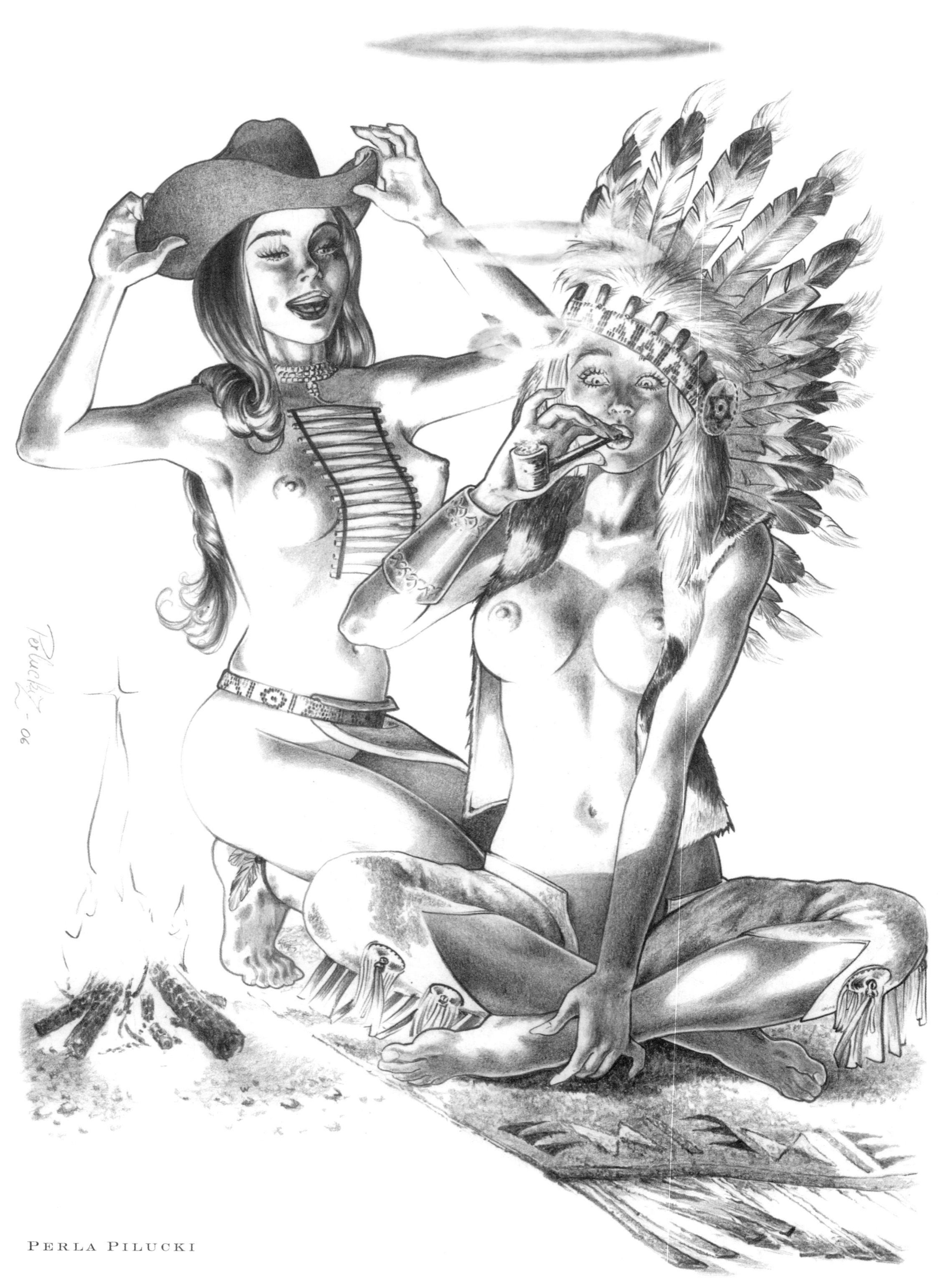

PERLA PILUCKI

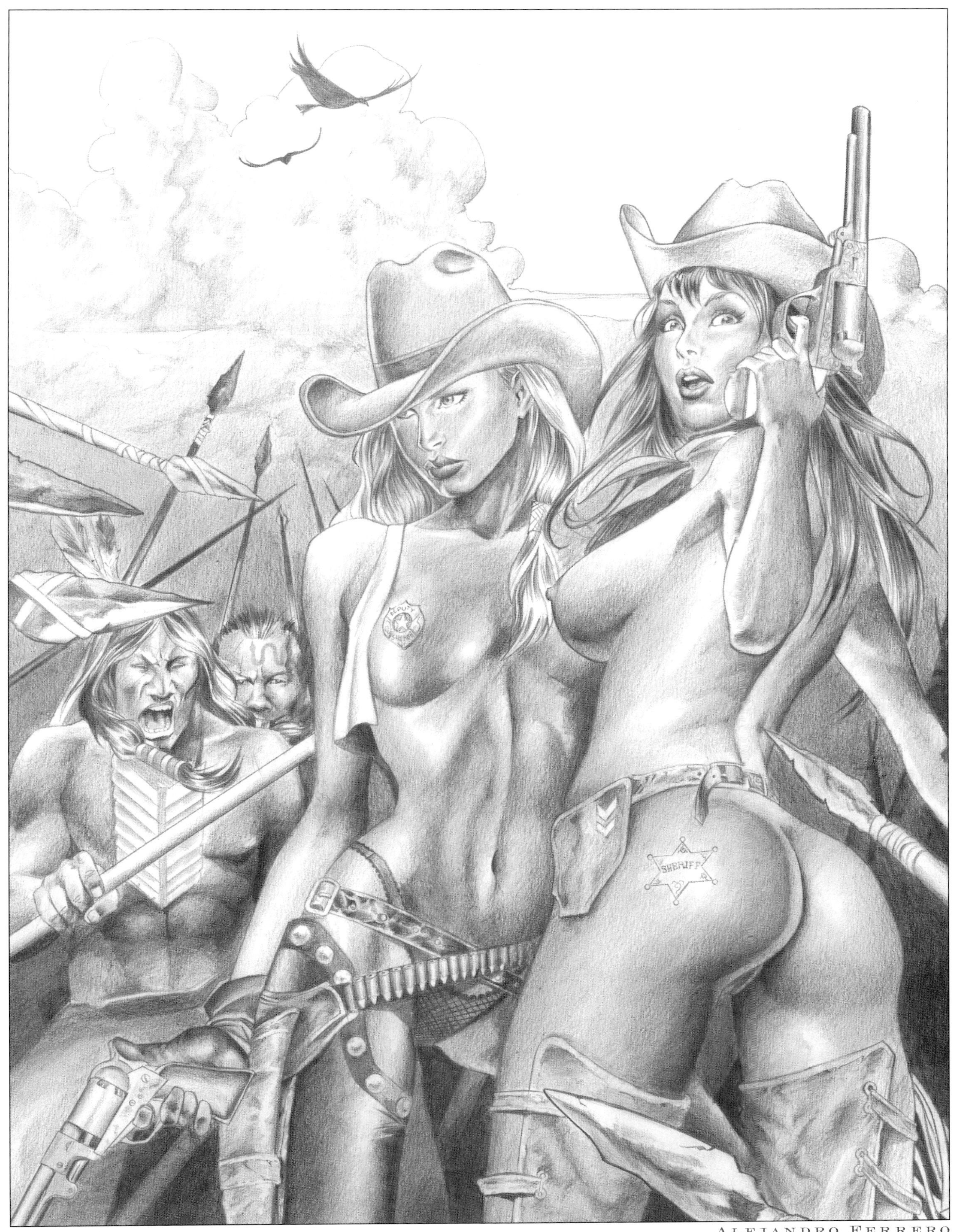

ALEJANDRO FERRERO

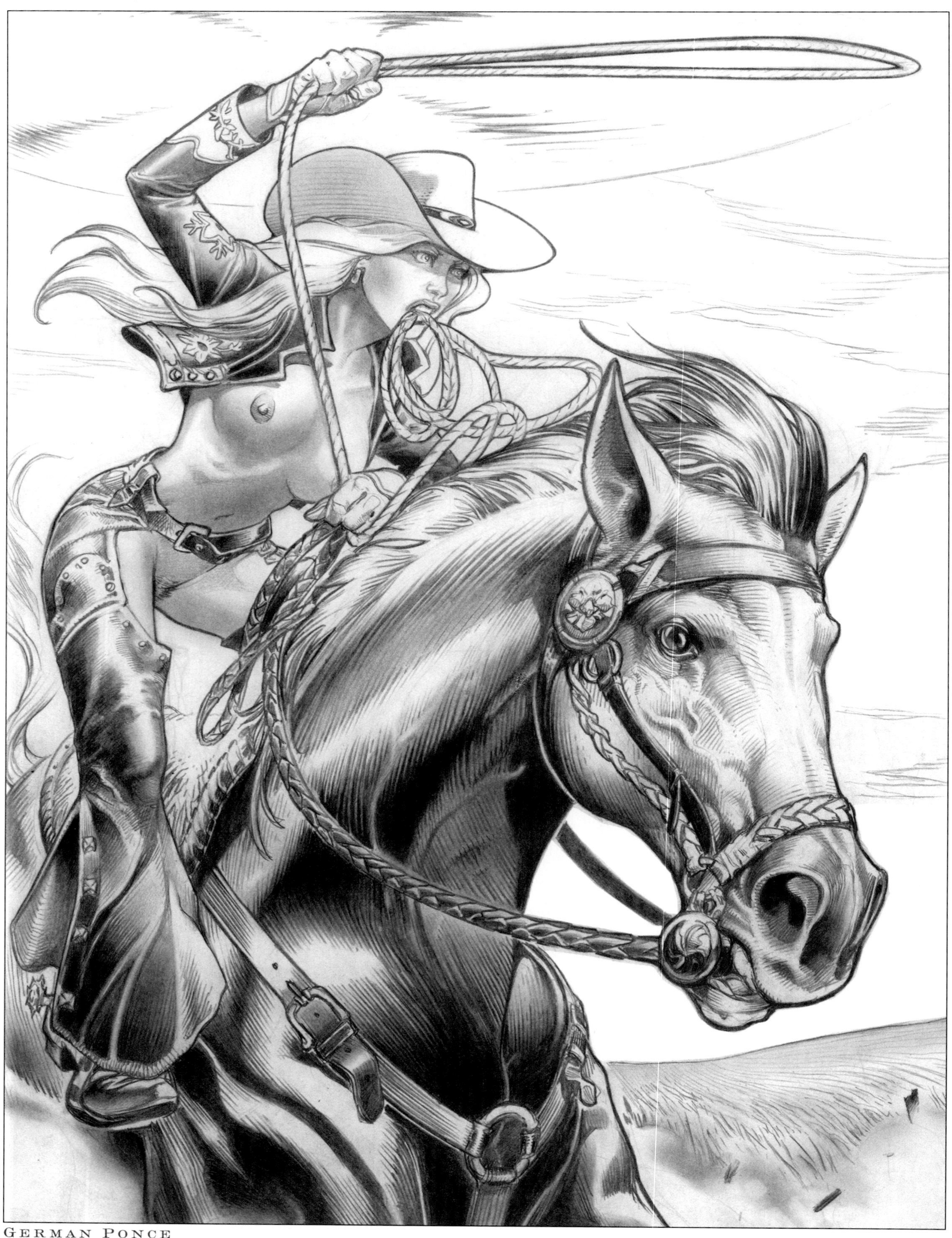

GERMAN PONCE

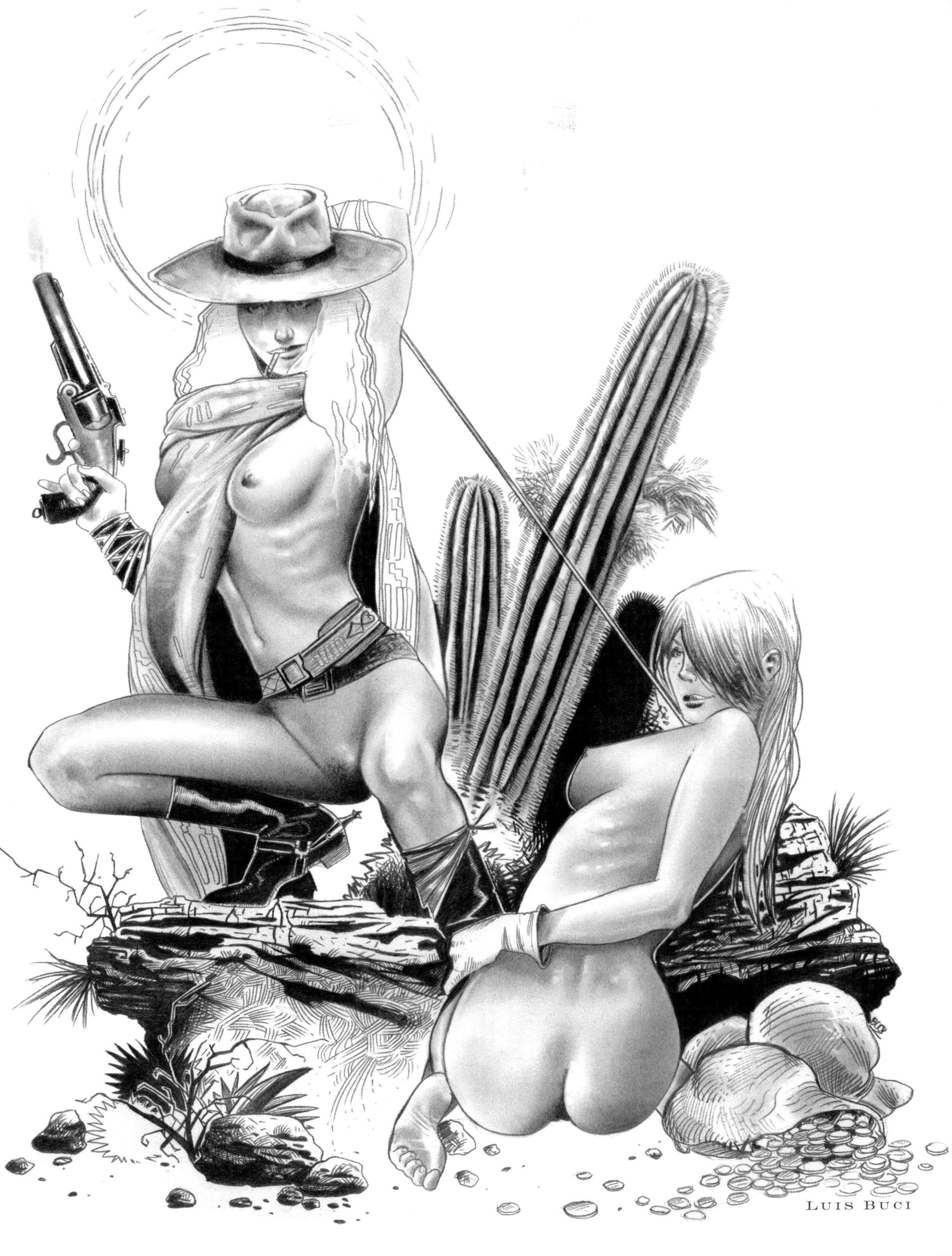

LUIS BUCI

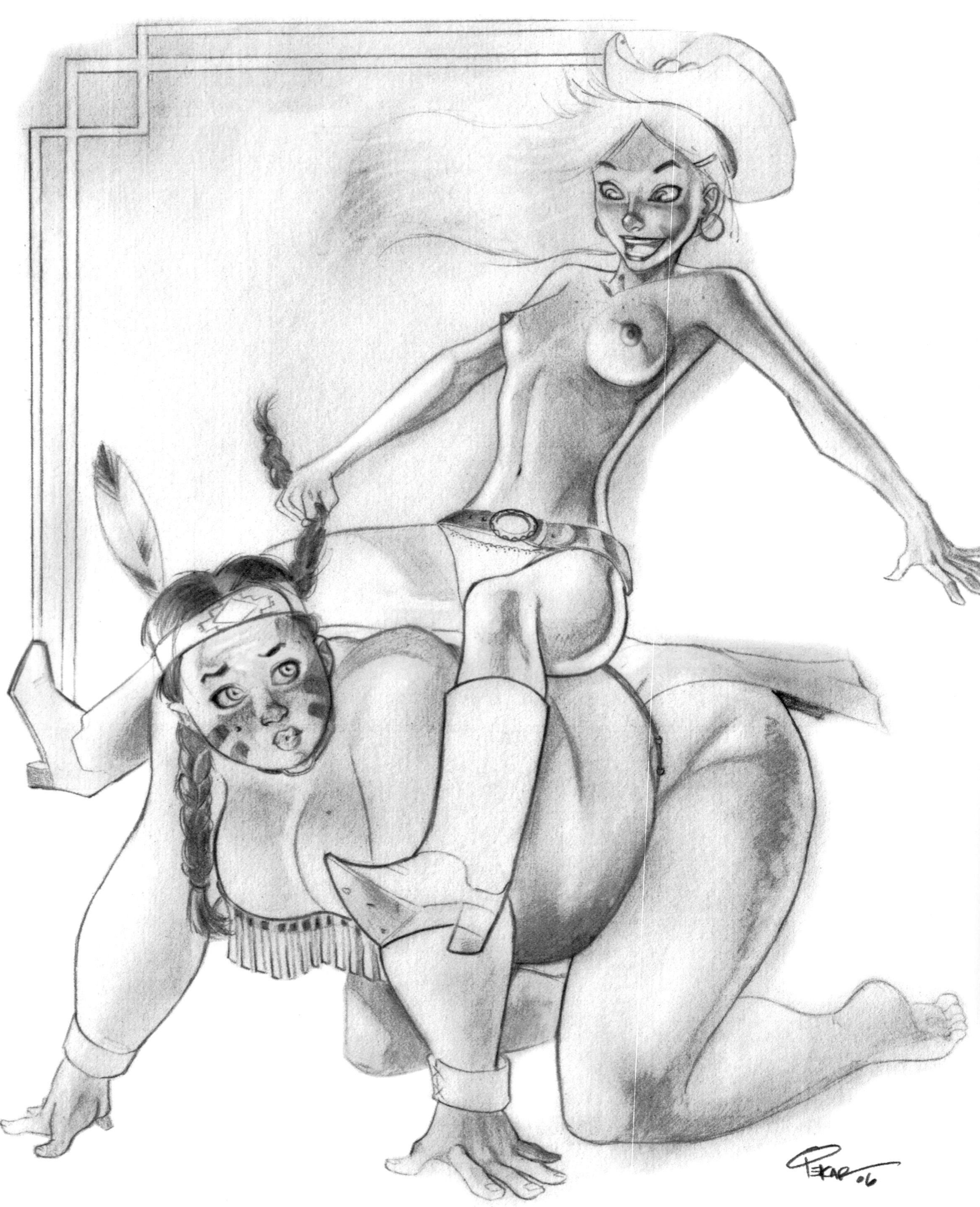

Joe Pekar

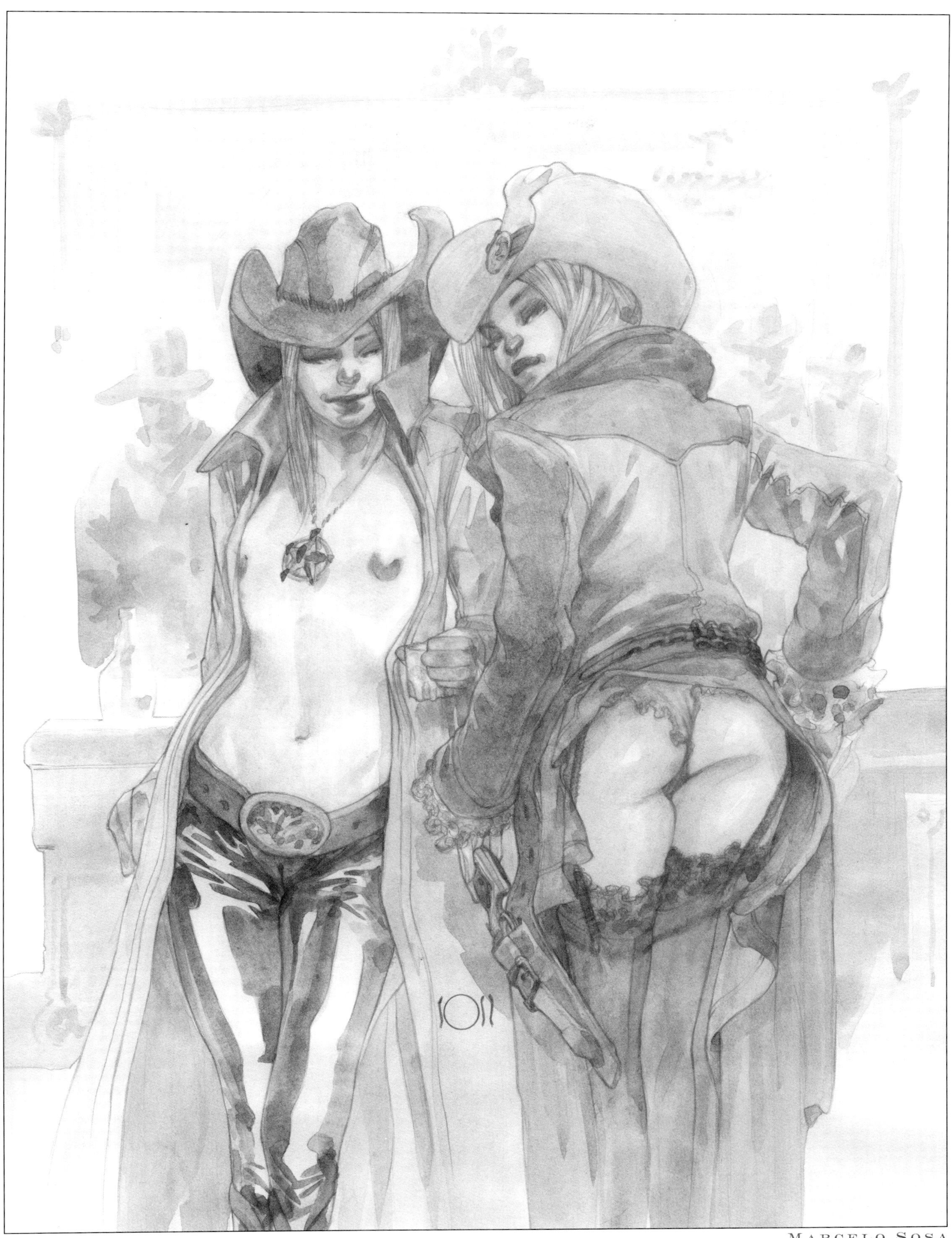

Marcelo Sosa

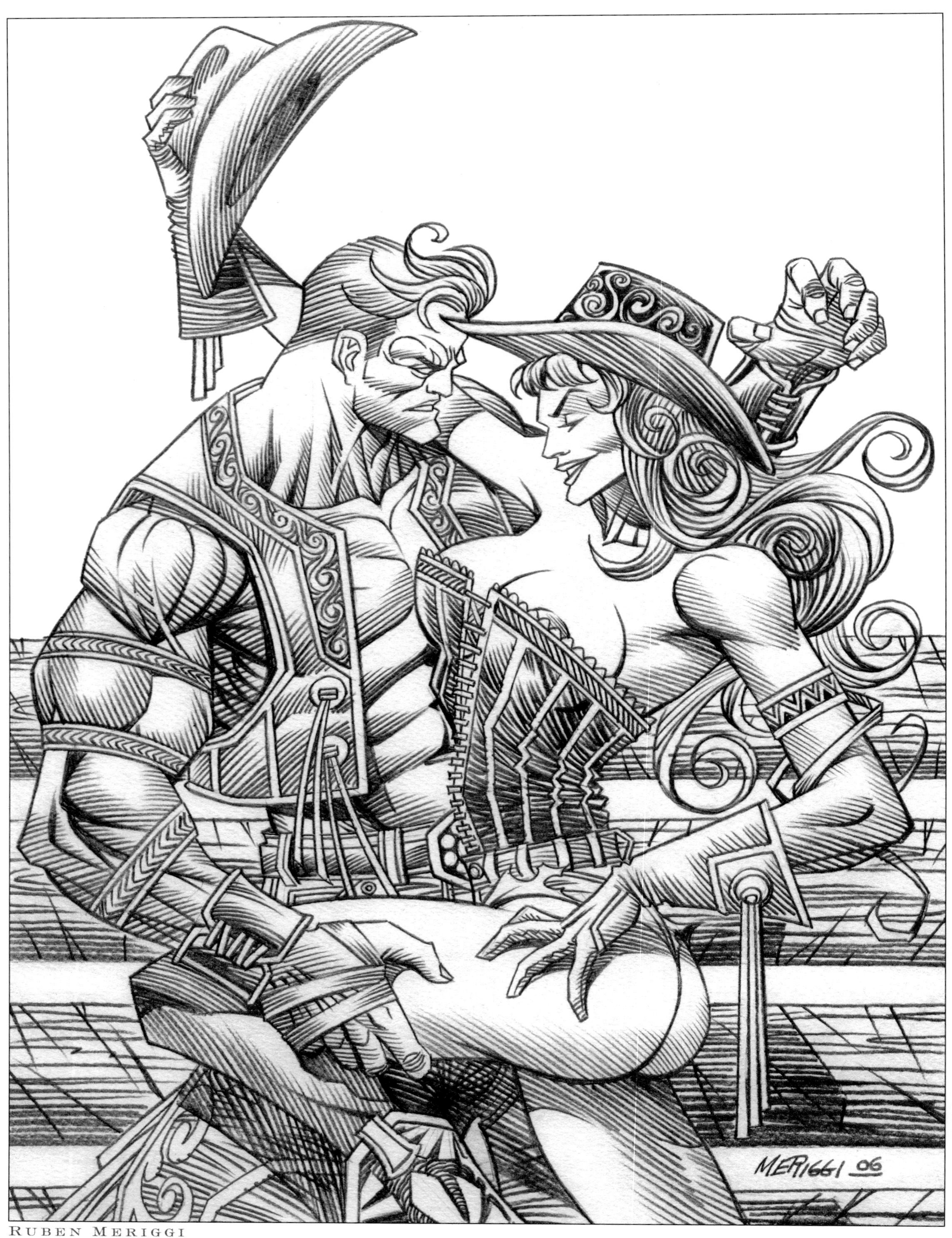

Ruben Meriggi

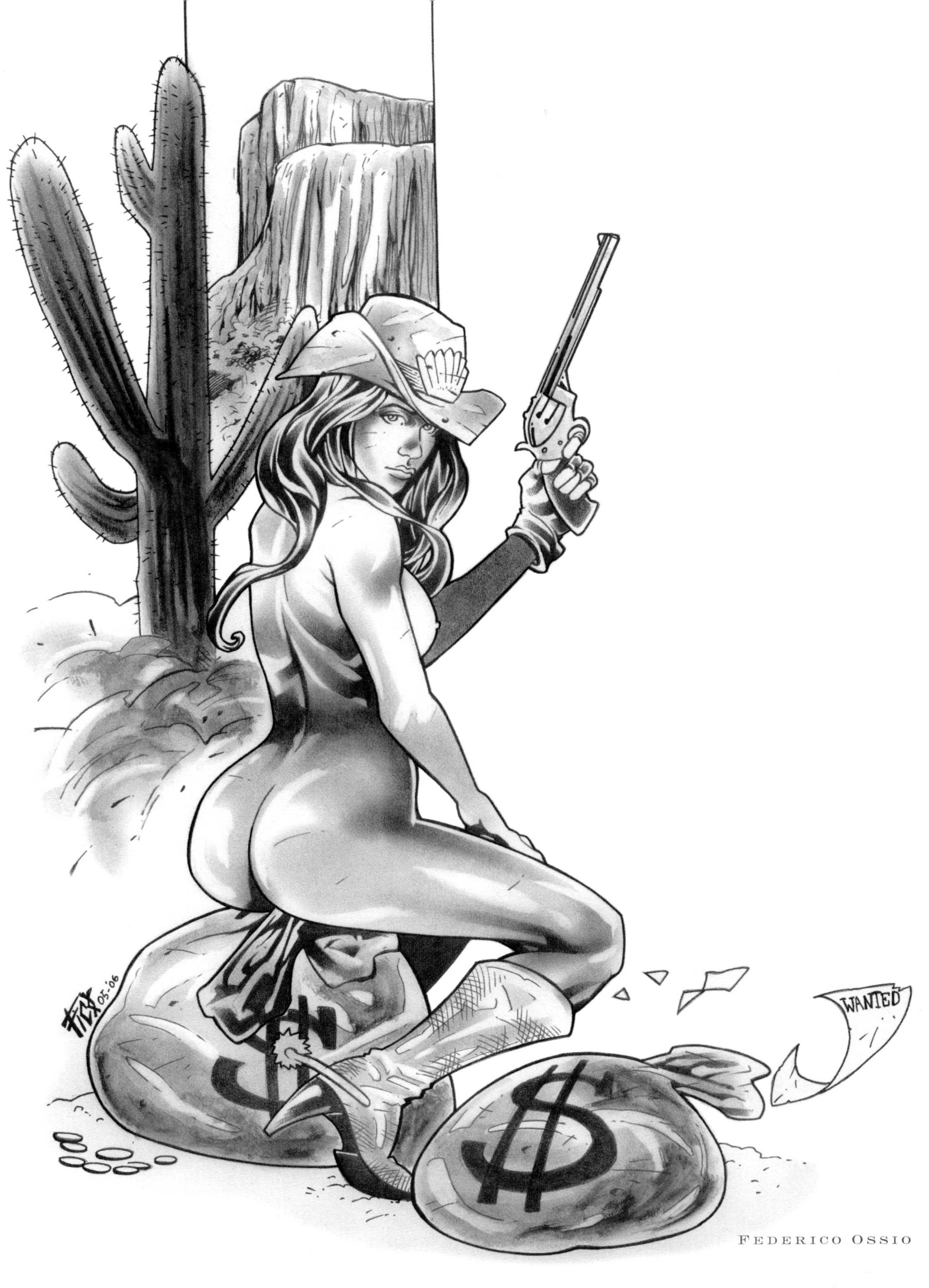

Federico Ossio

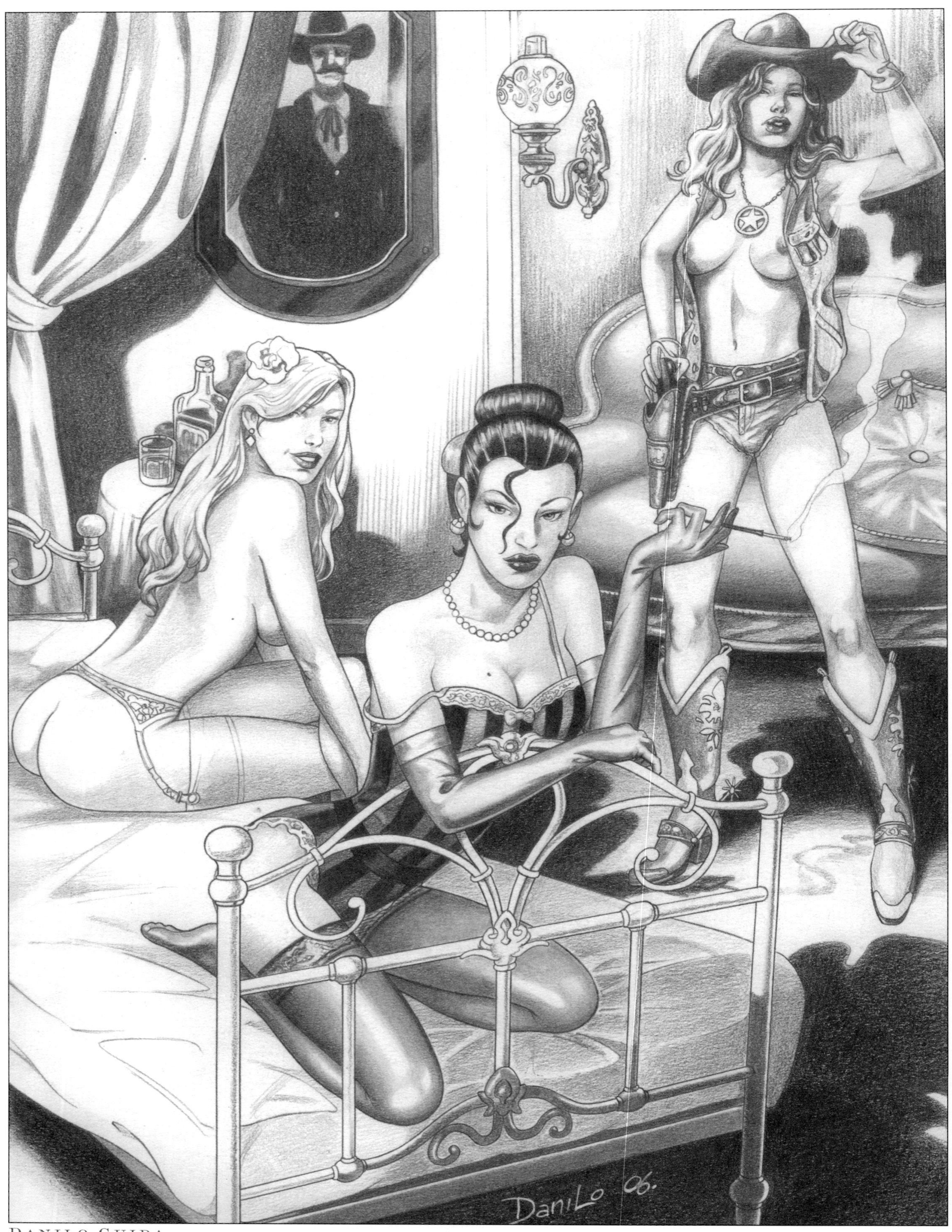

Danilo Guida

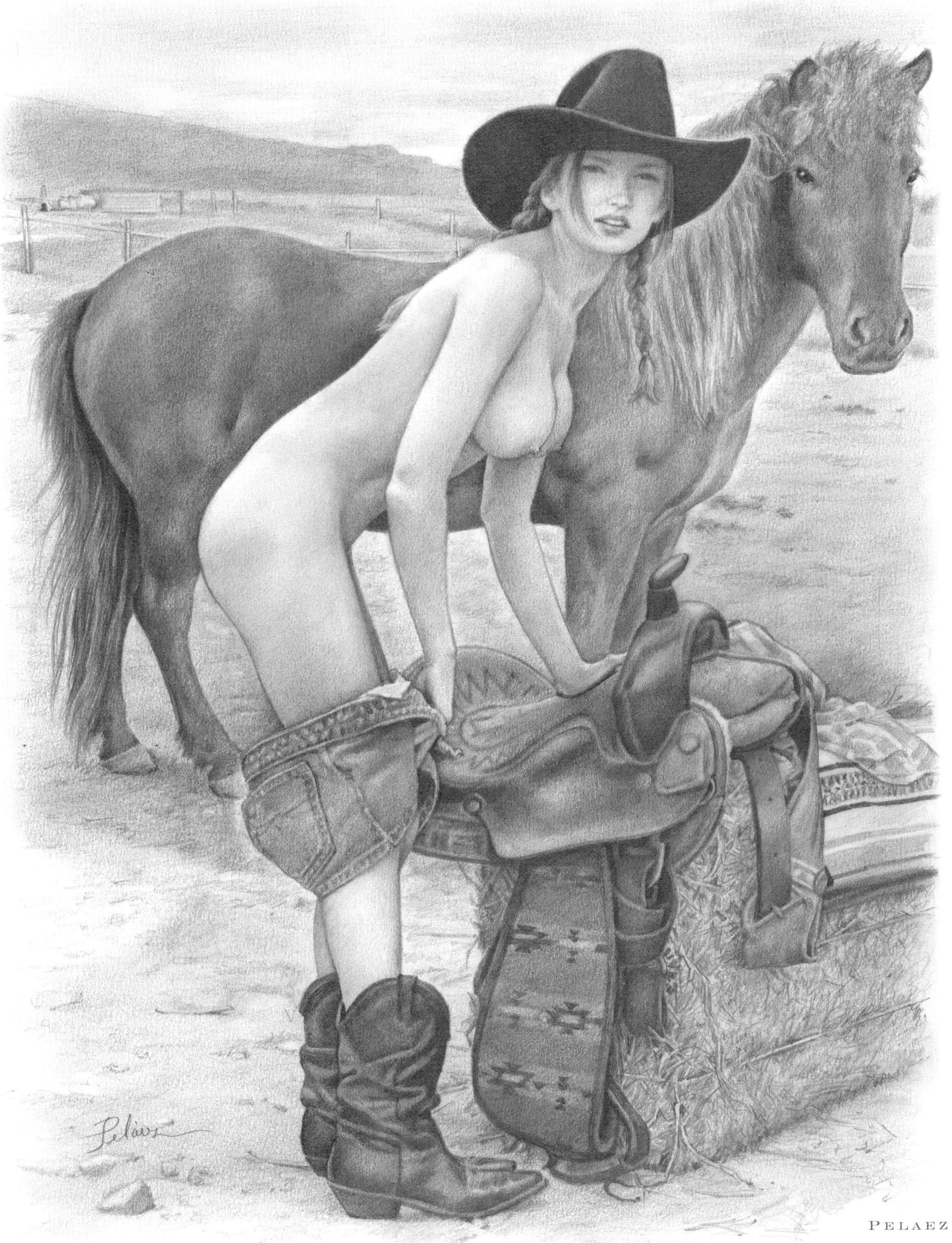

PELAEZ

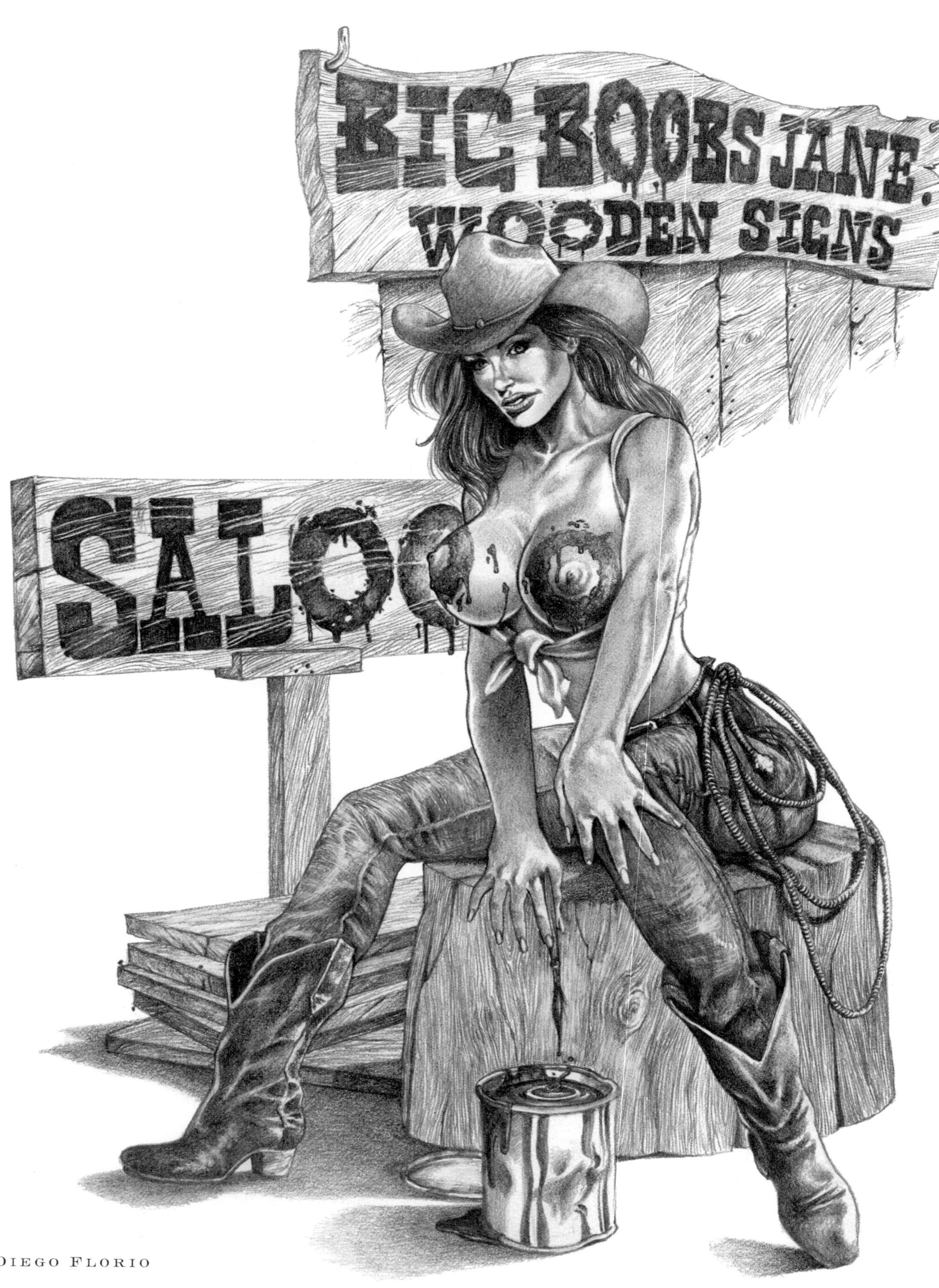

Diego Florio

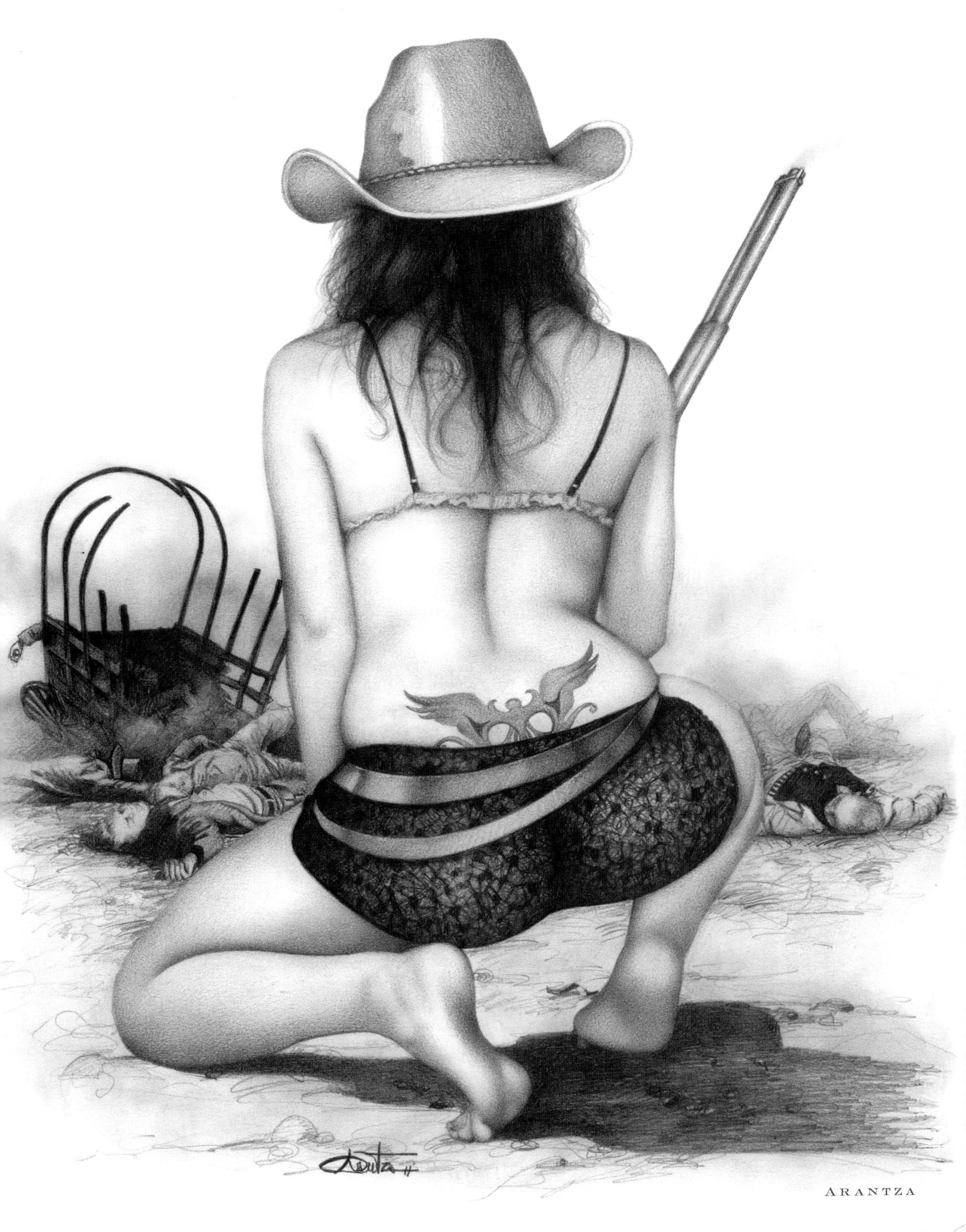

Arantza

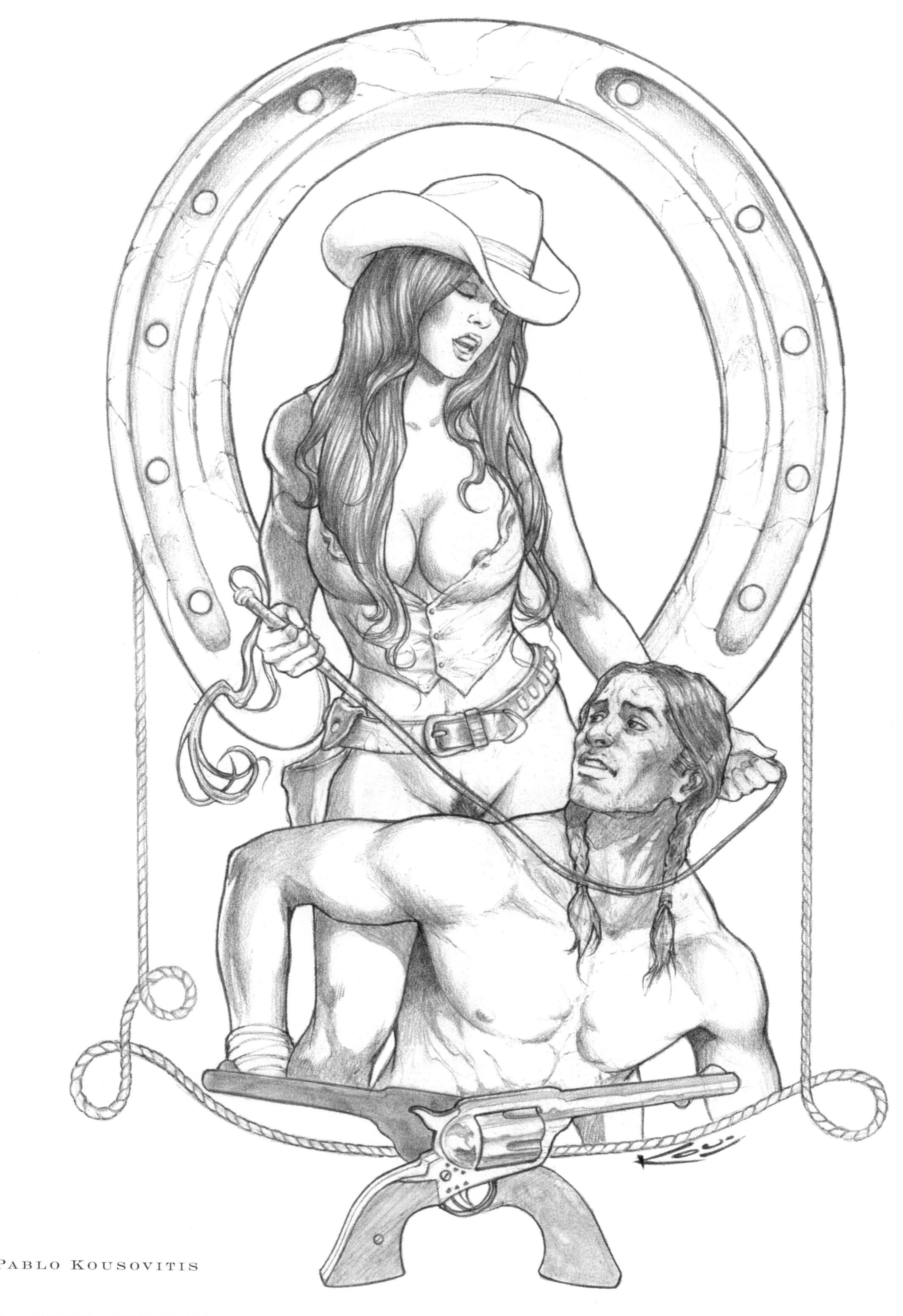

Pablo Kousovitis

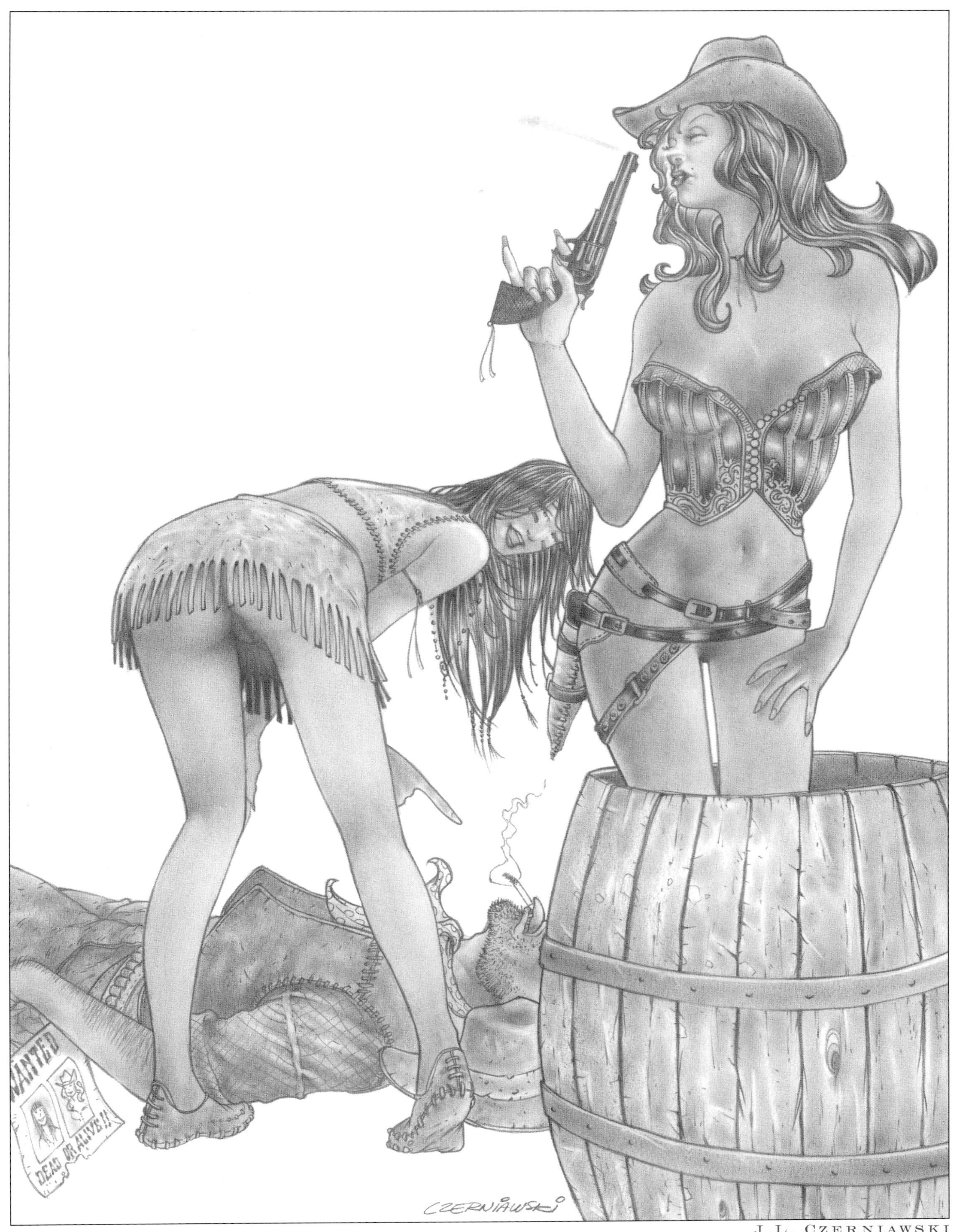

J.L. CZERNIAWSKI

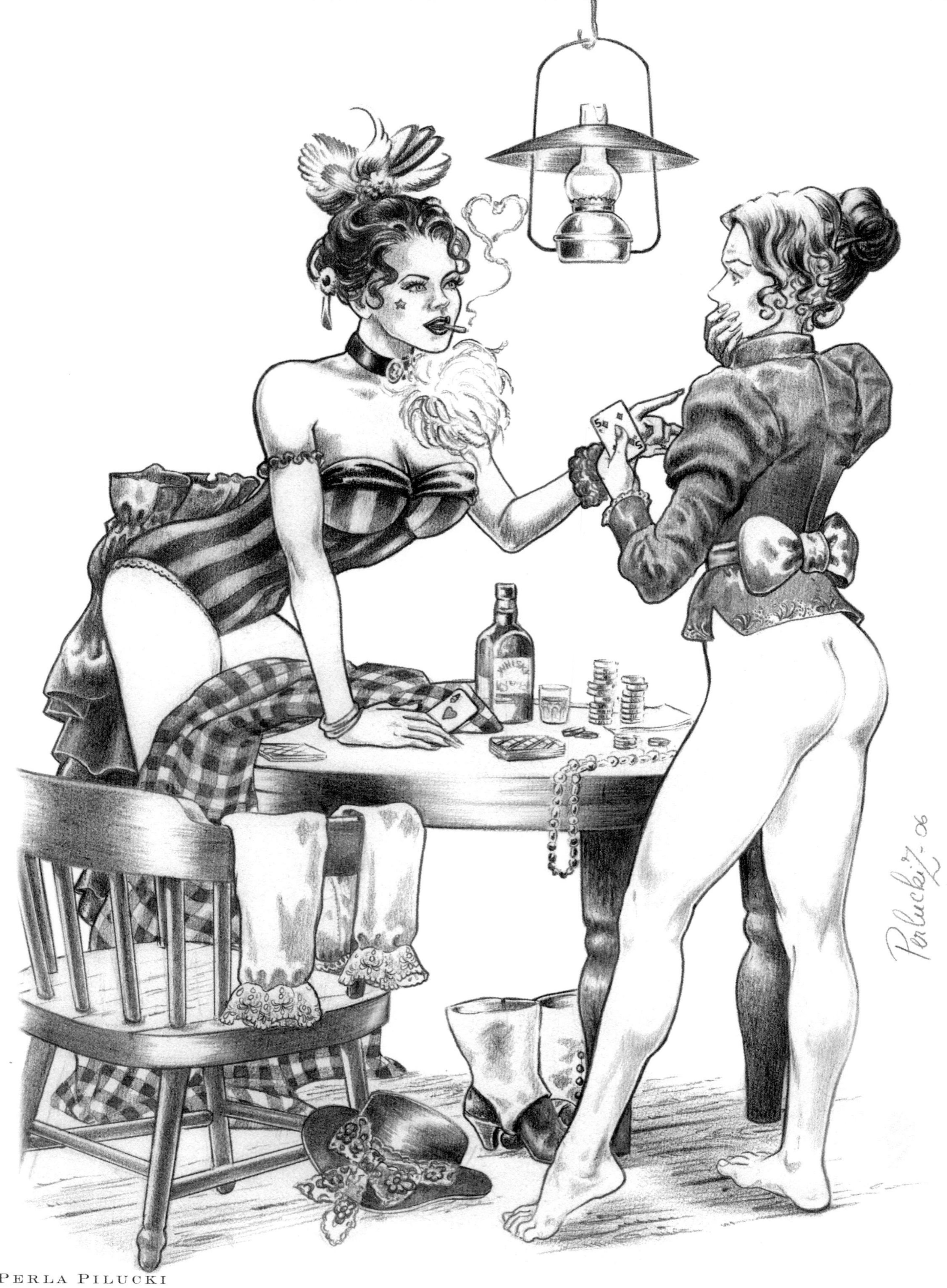

Perla Pilucki

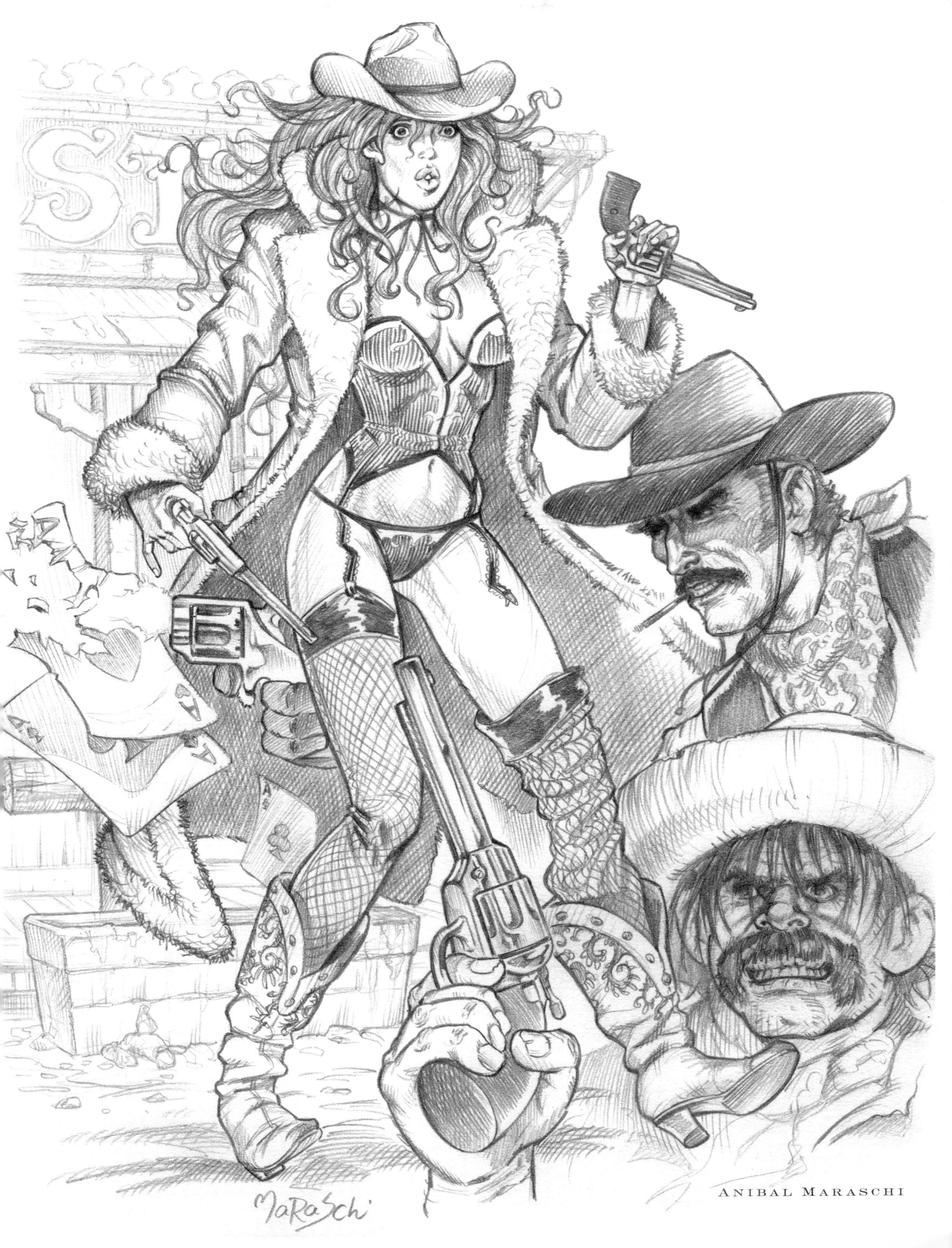

ANIBAL MARASCHI

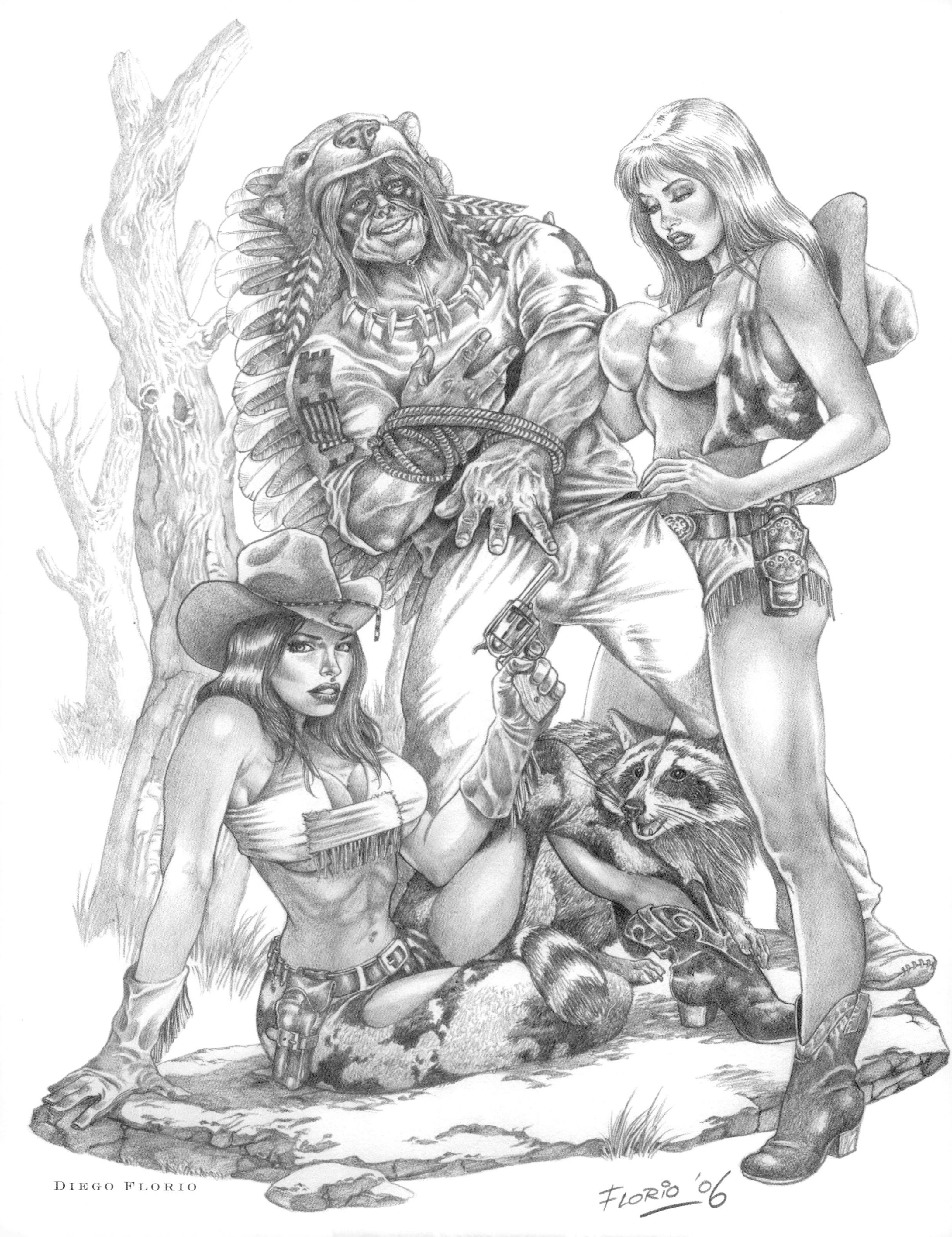

DIEGO FLORIO

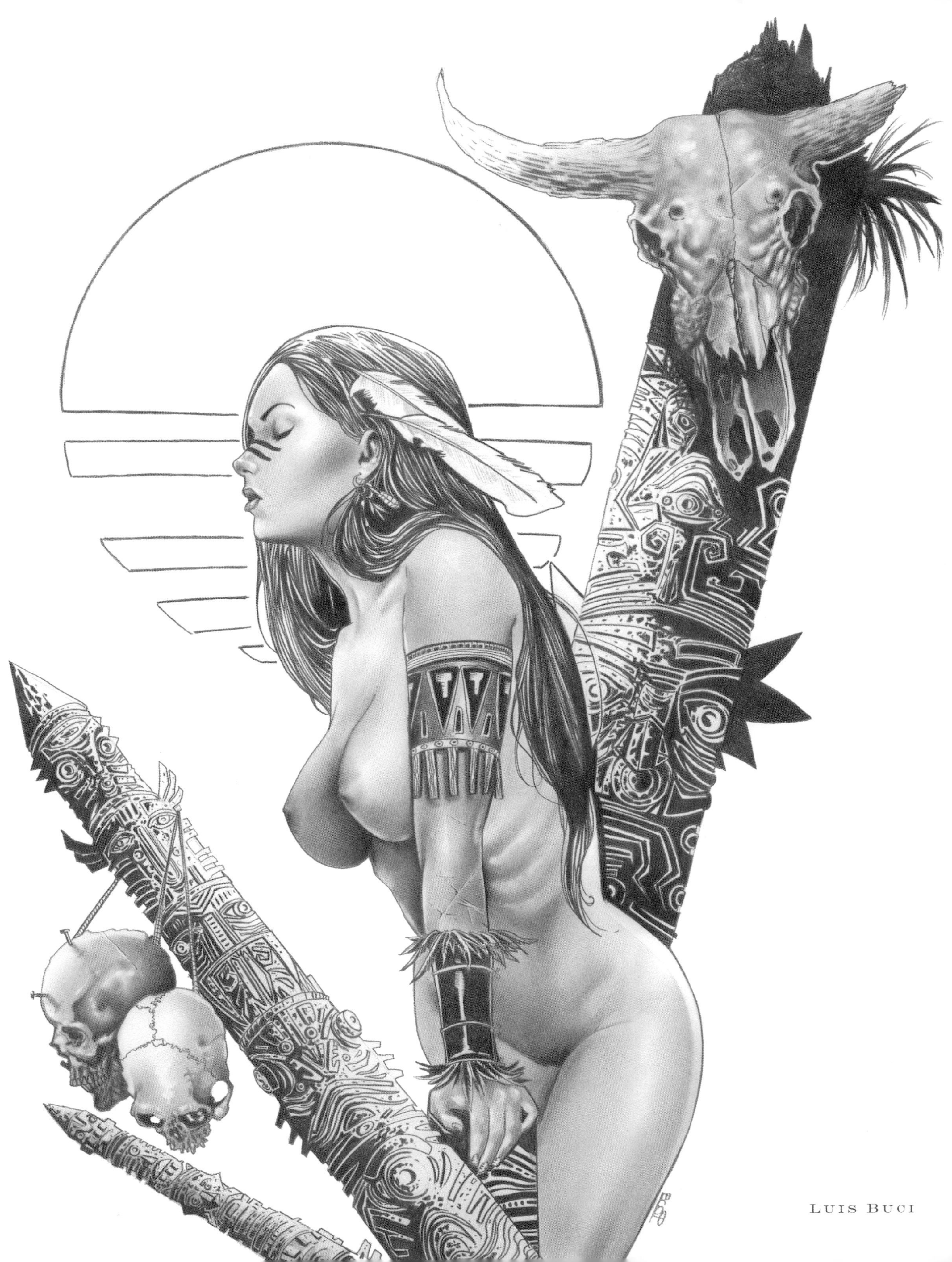

Luis Buci

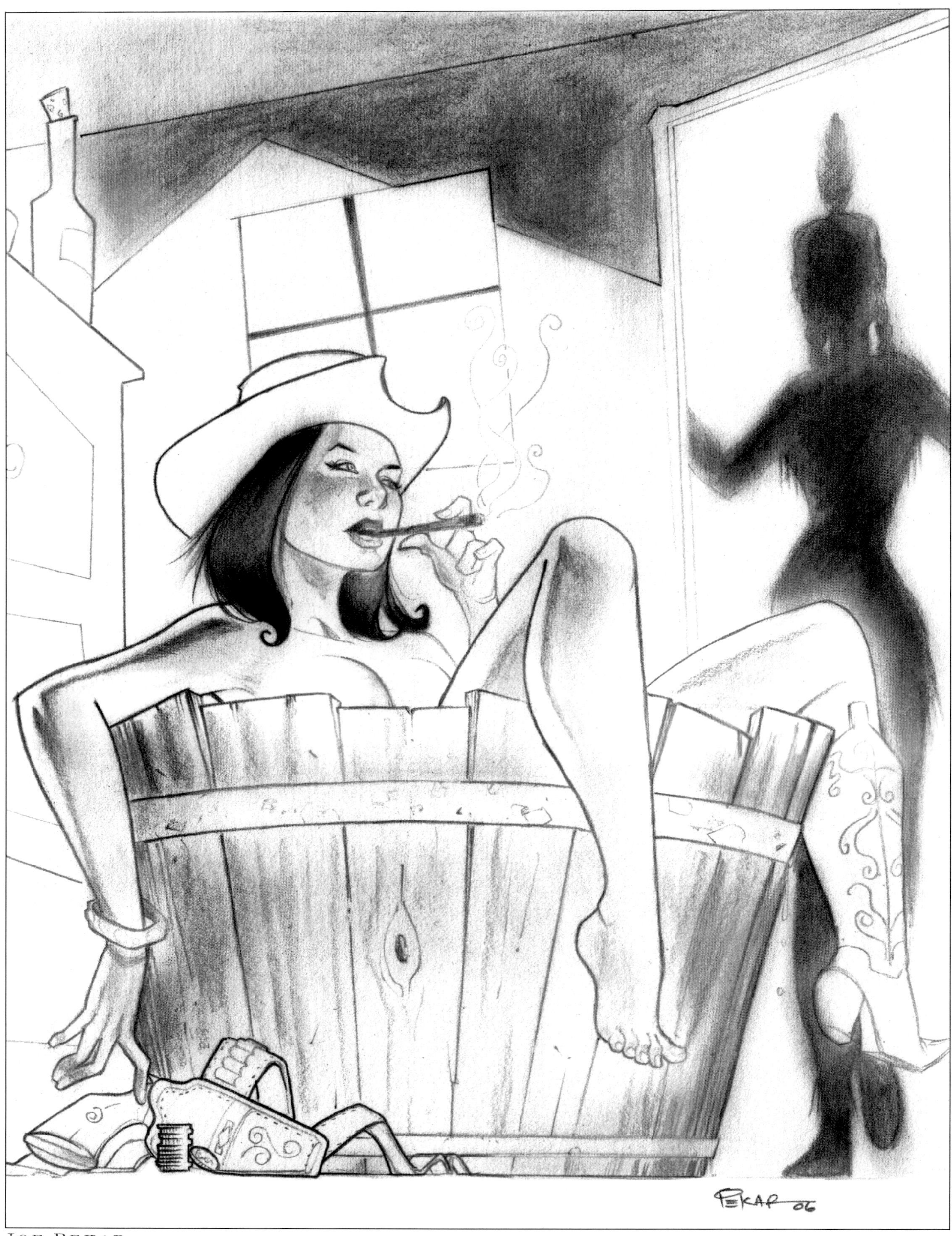

JOE PEKAR

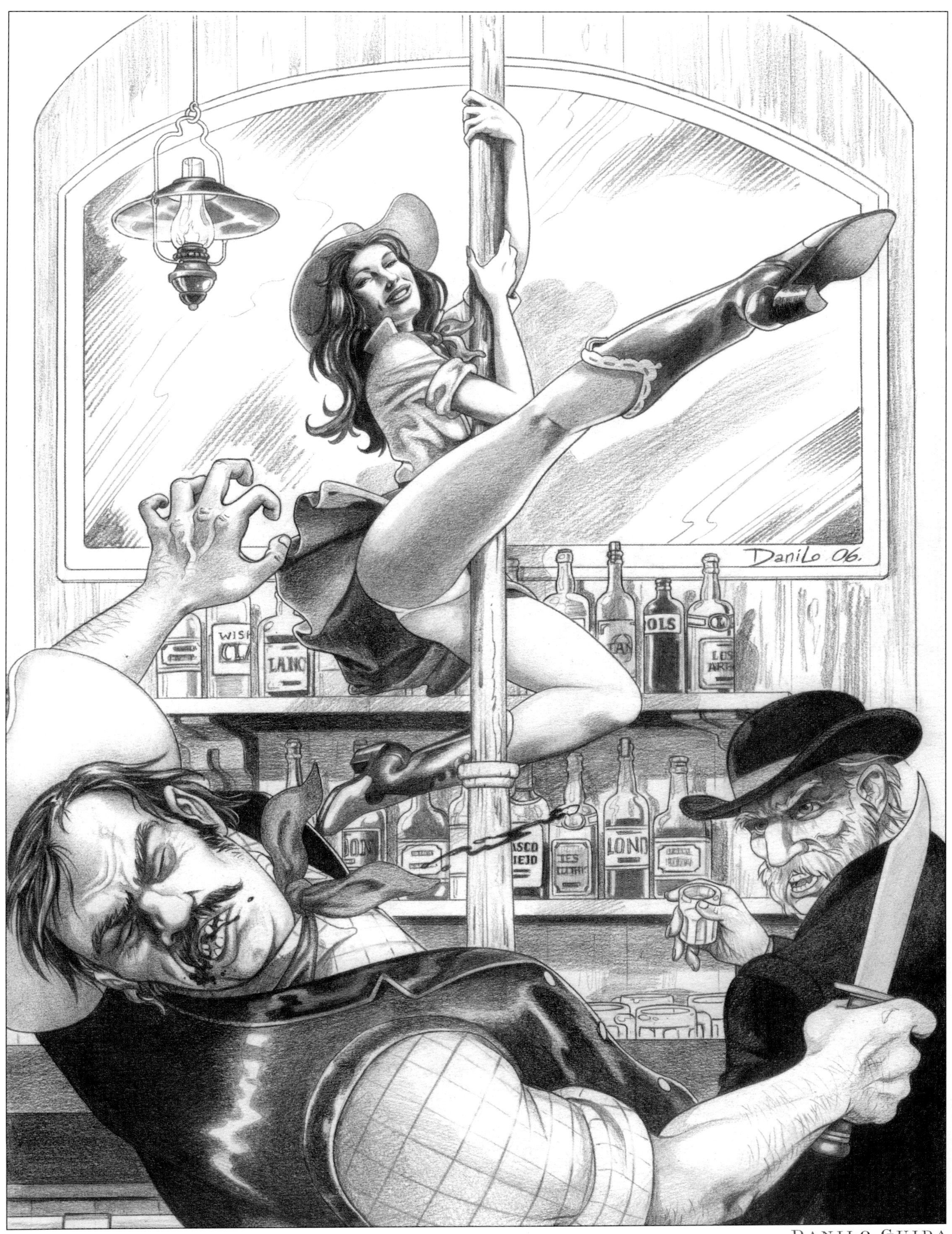

DANILO GUIDA

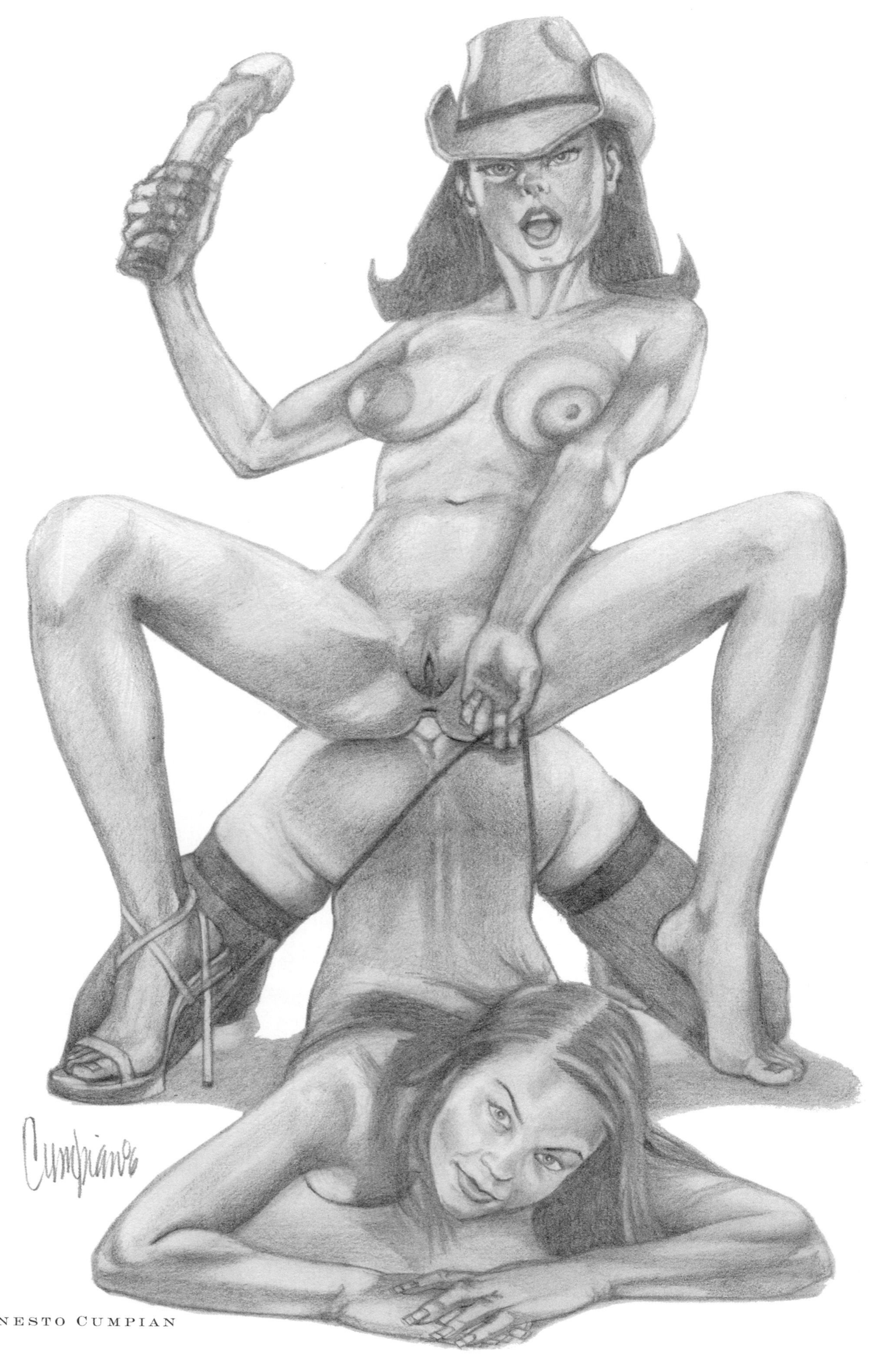

Ernesto Cumpian

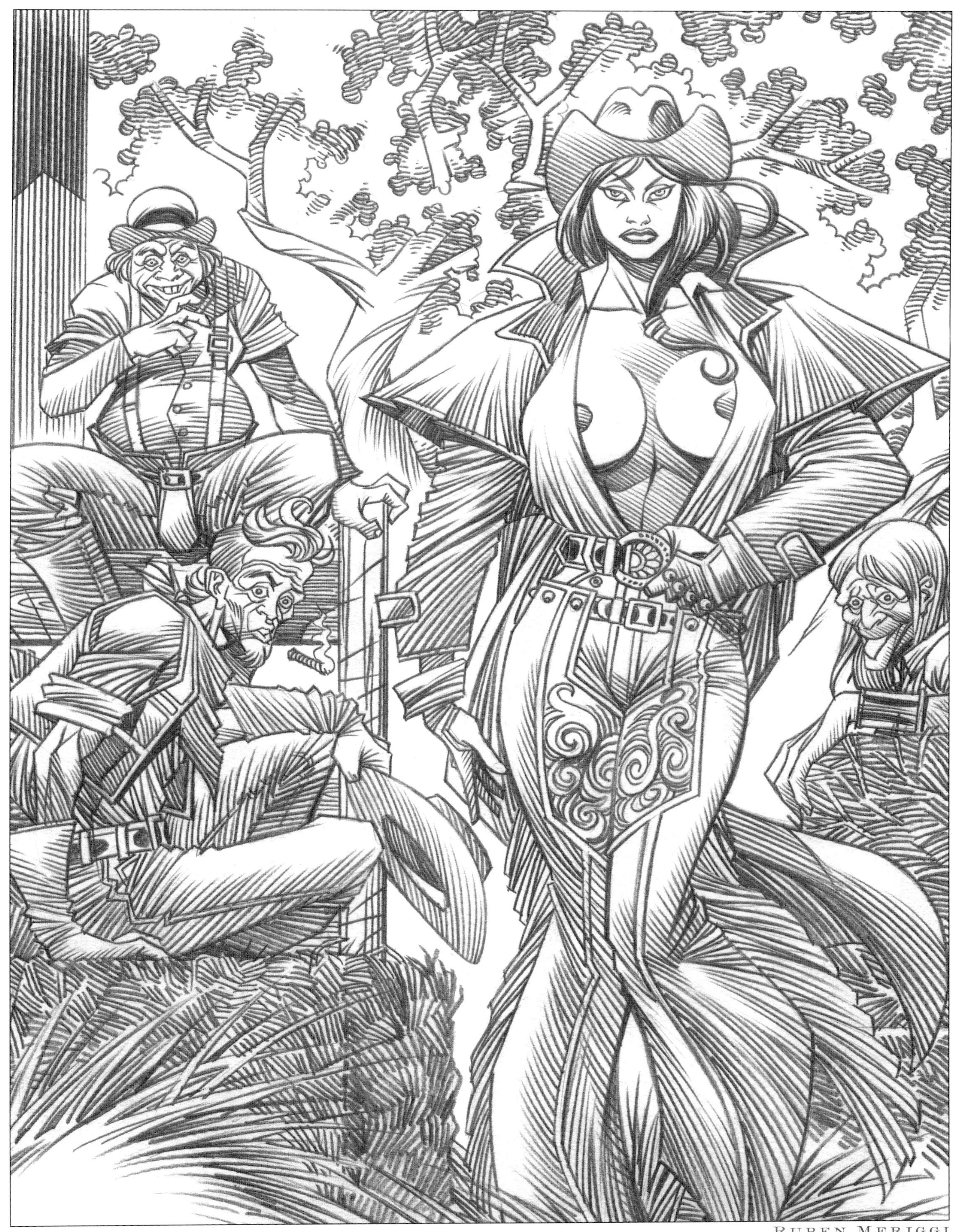

Ruben Meriggi

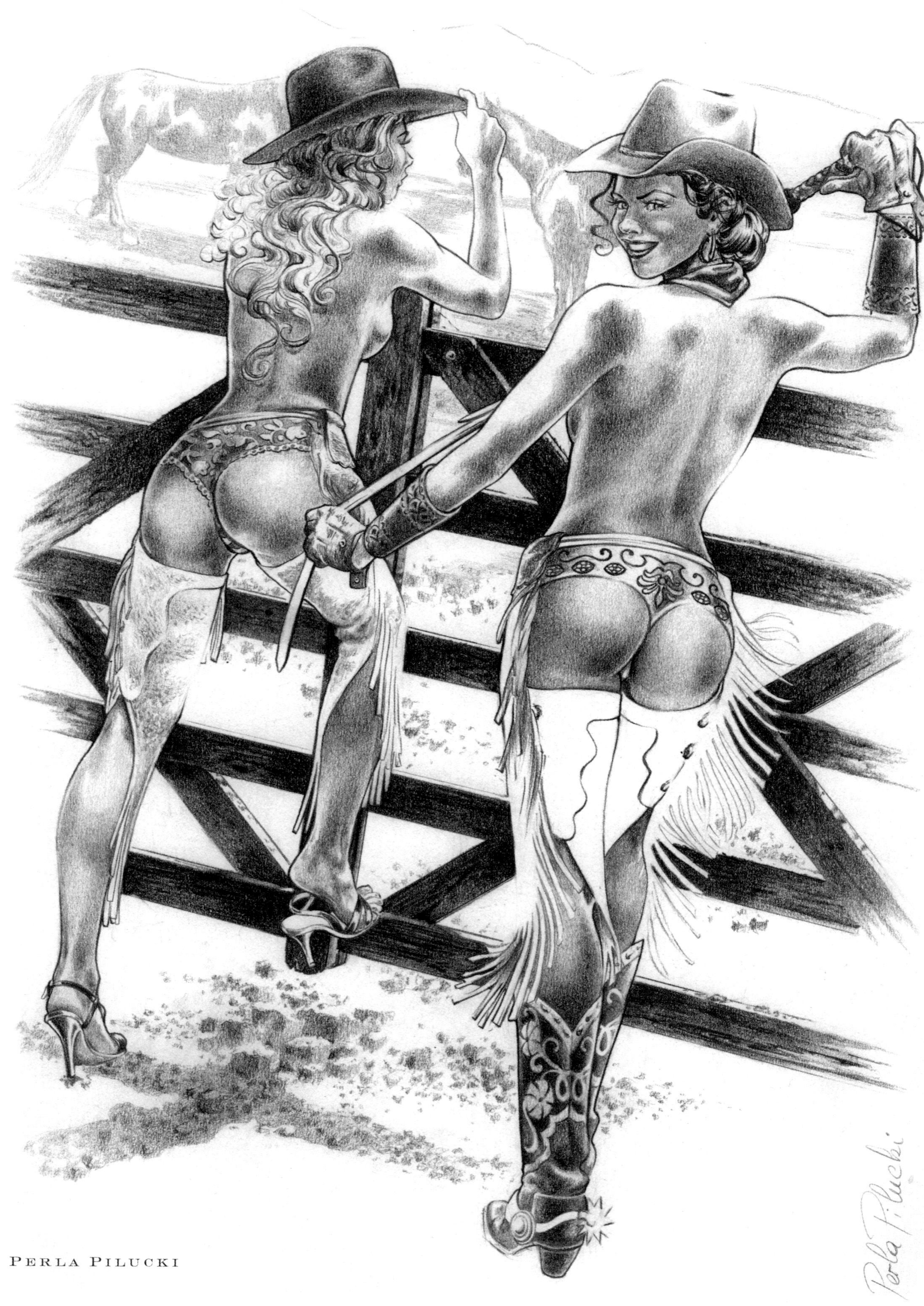

Perla Pilucki

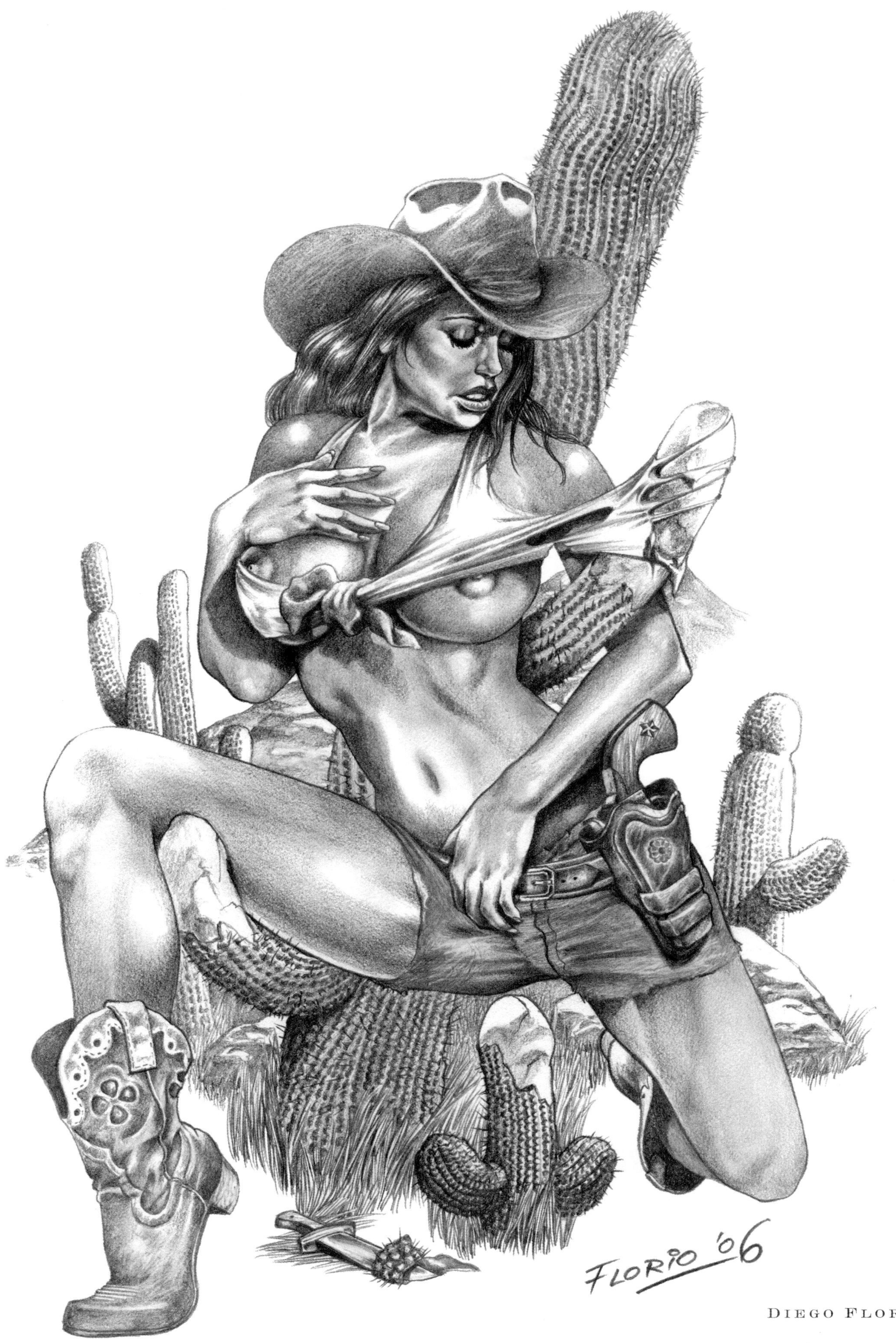

DIEGO FLORIO

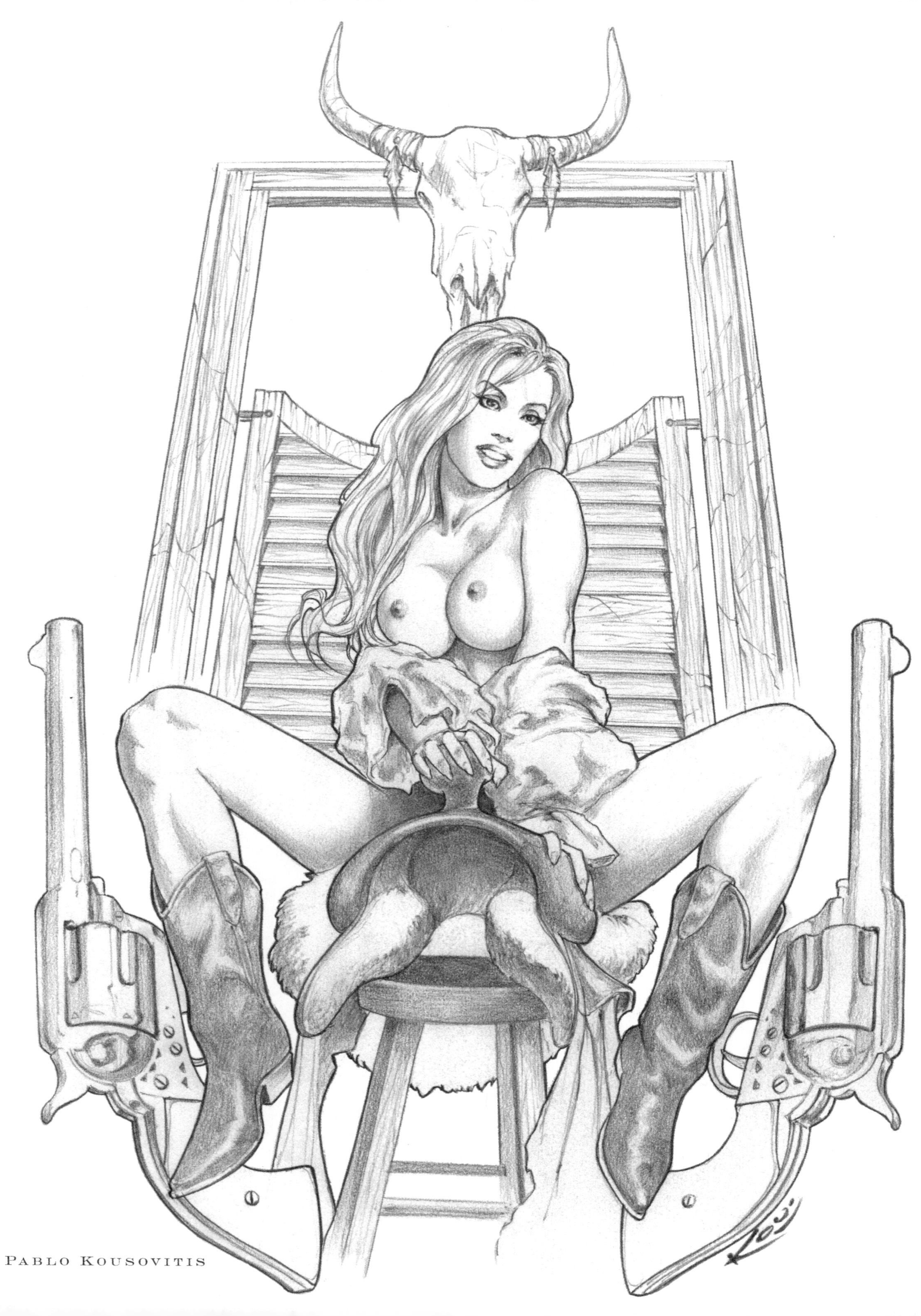

Pablo Kousovitis

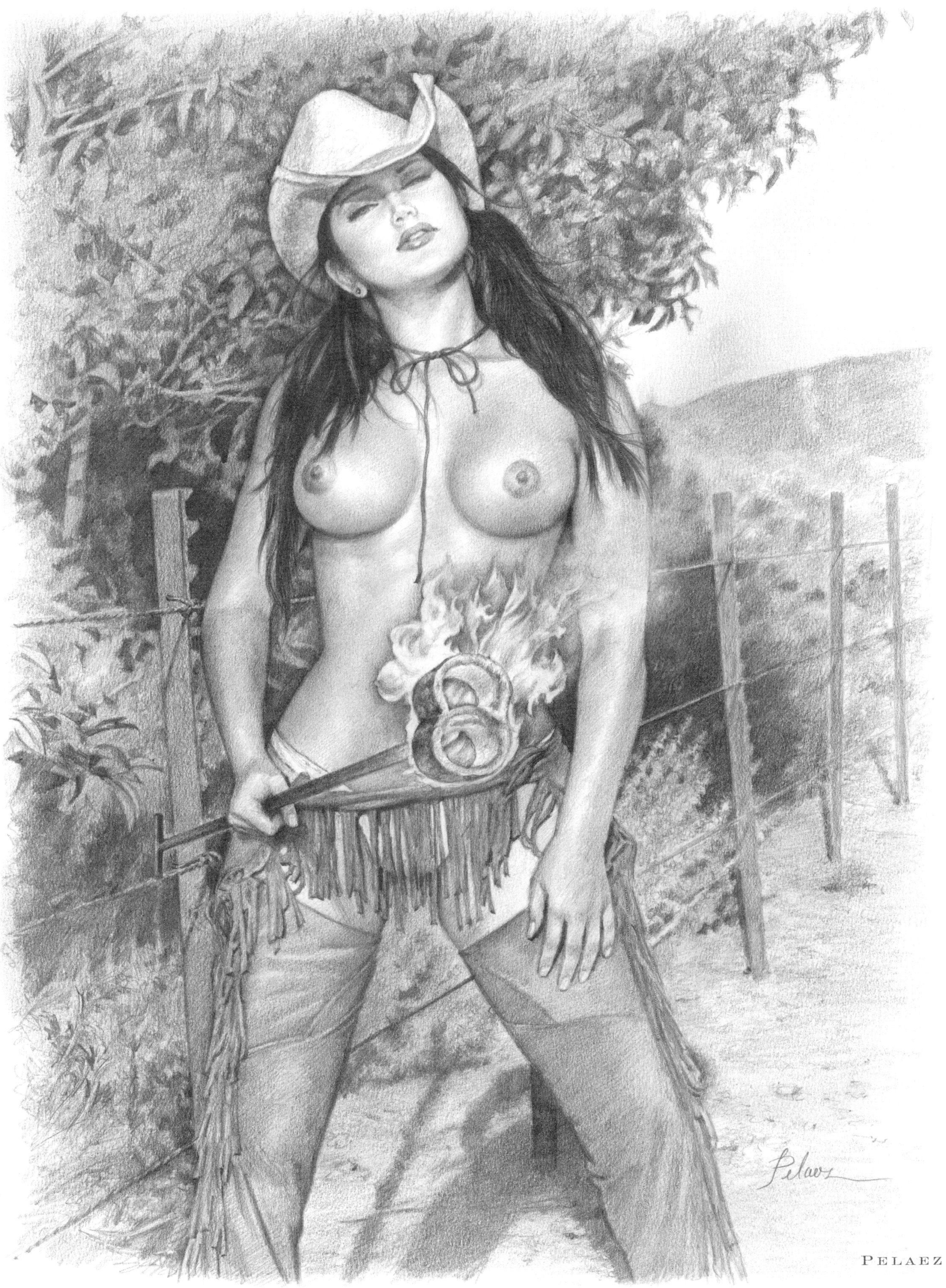

PELAEZ

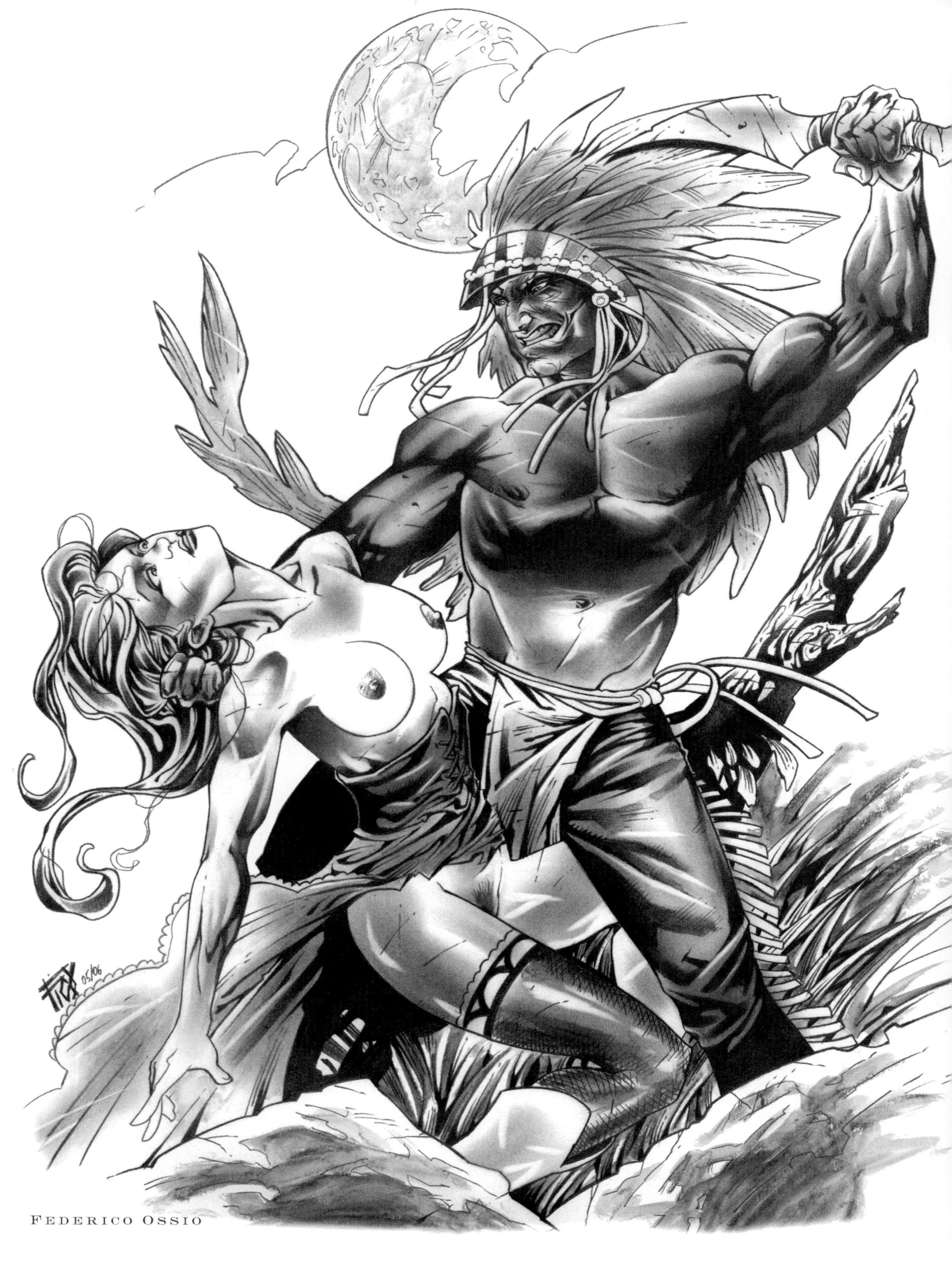

Federico Ossio

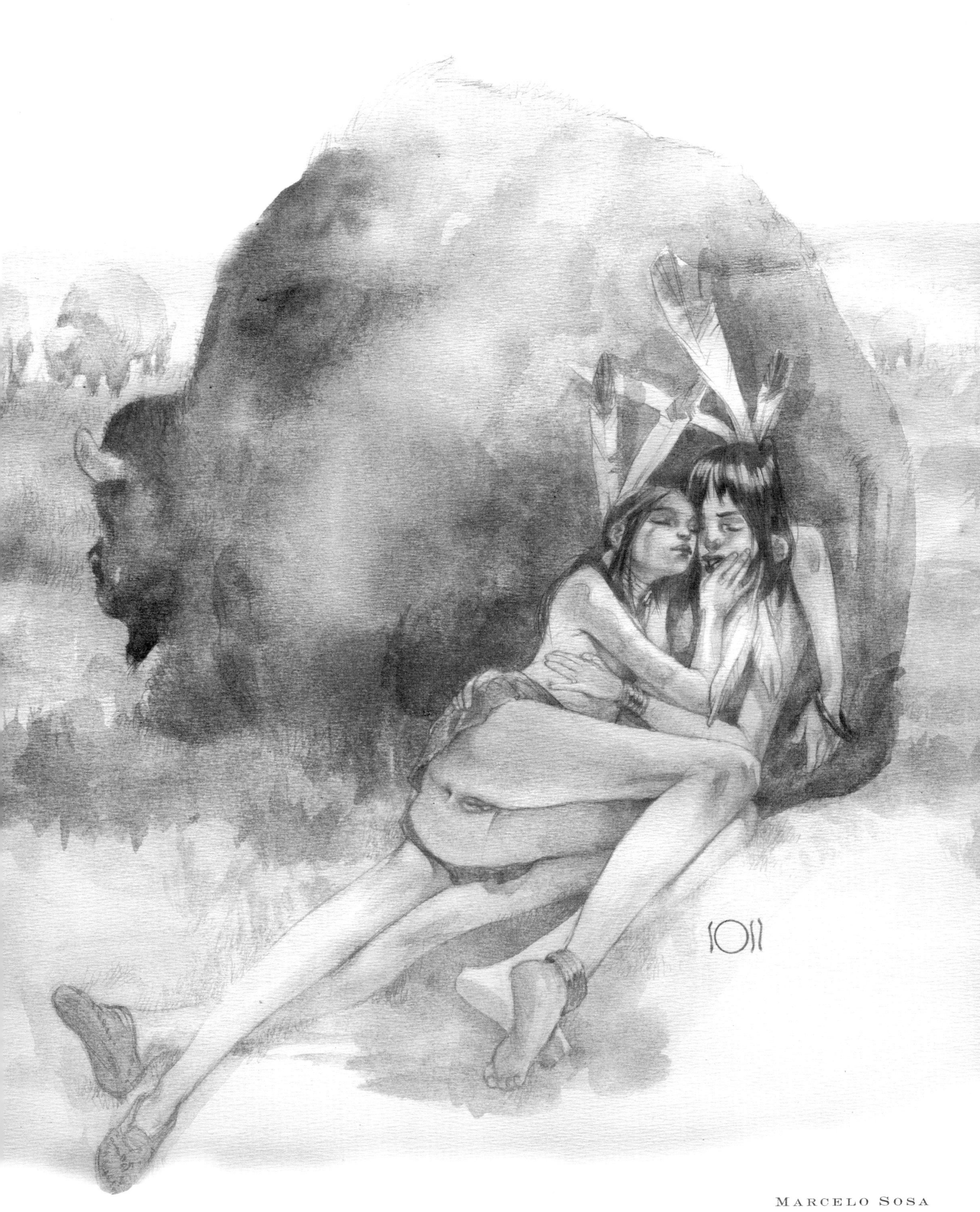

Marcelo Sosa

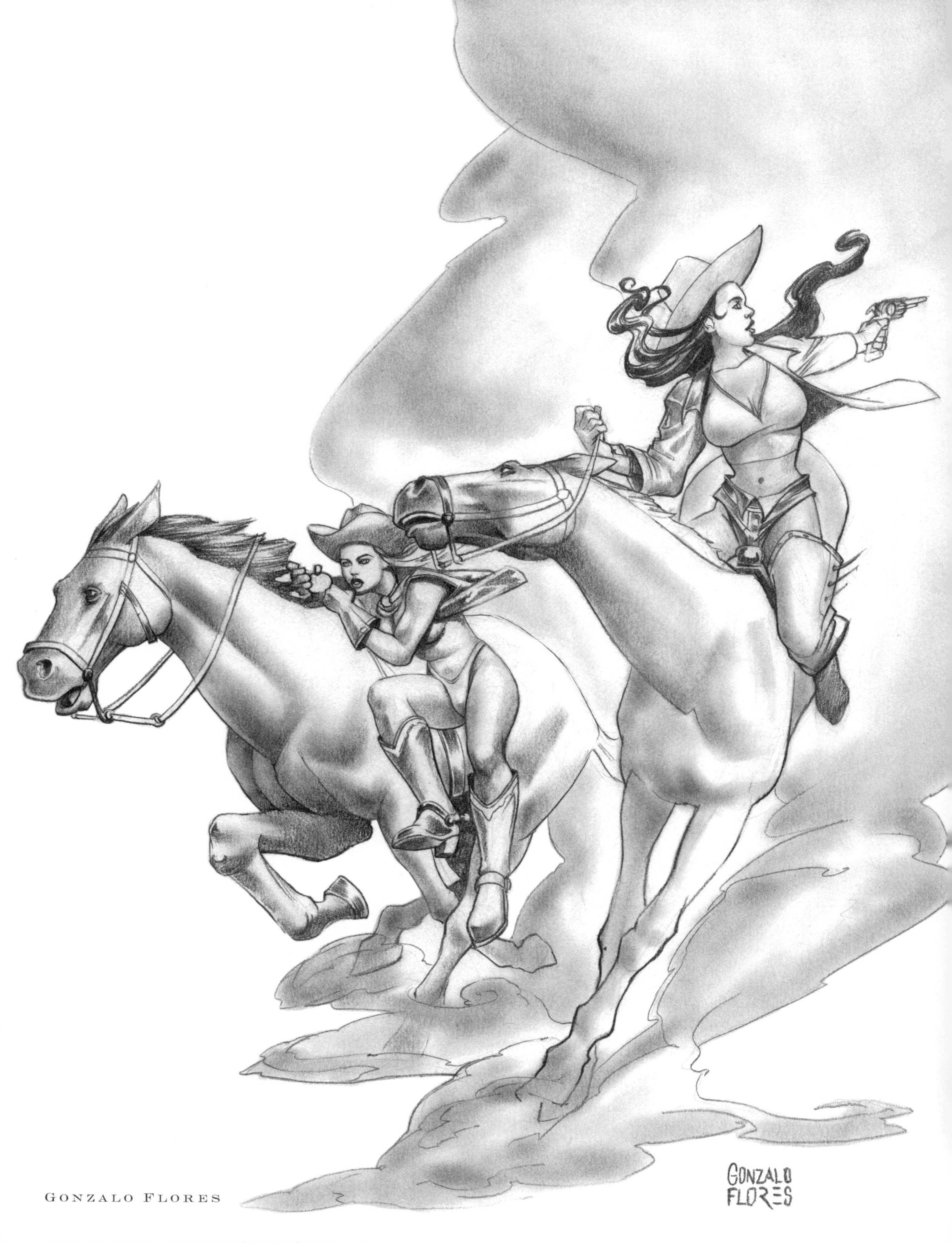

Gonzalo Flores

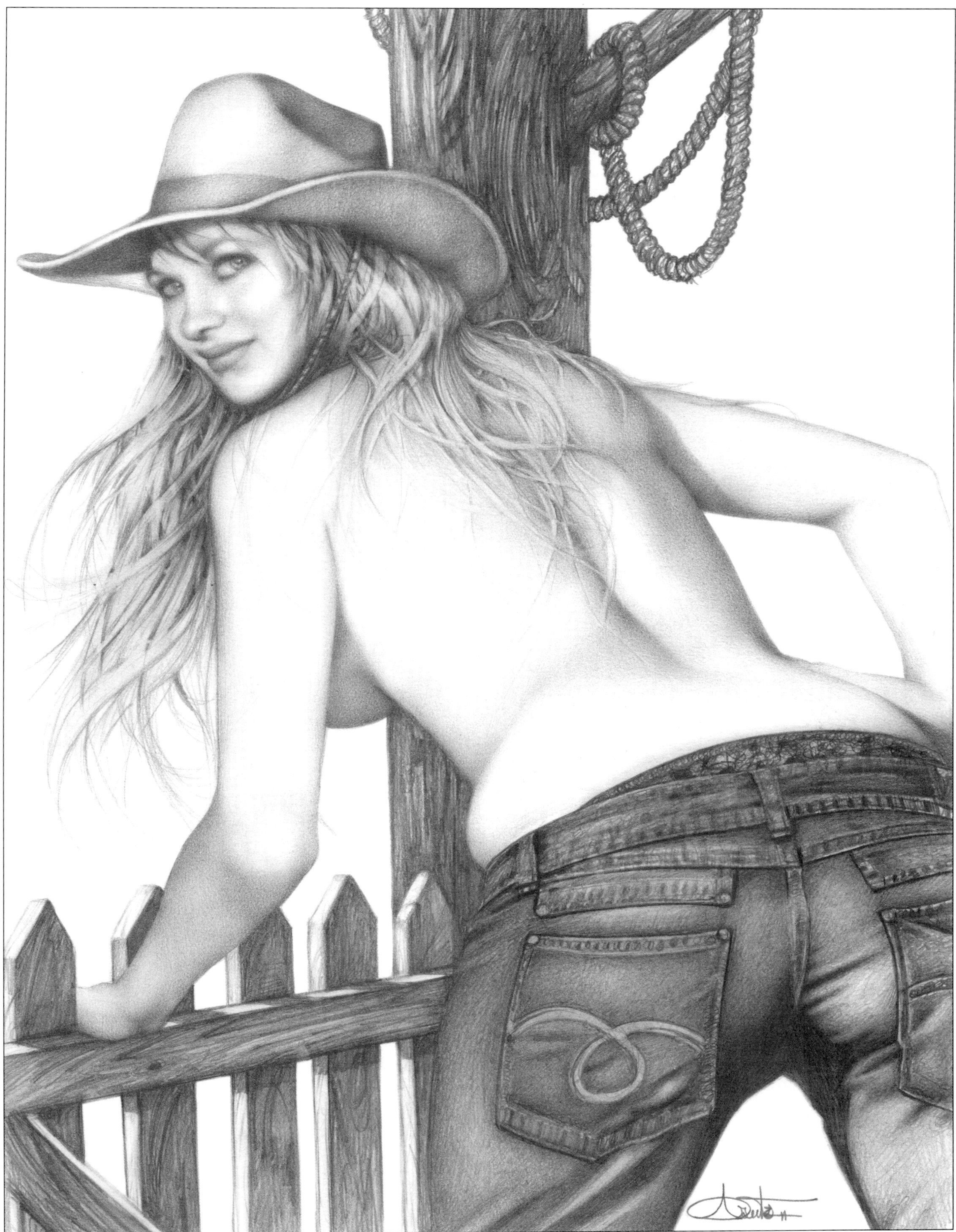

ARANTZA

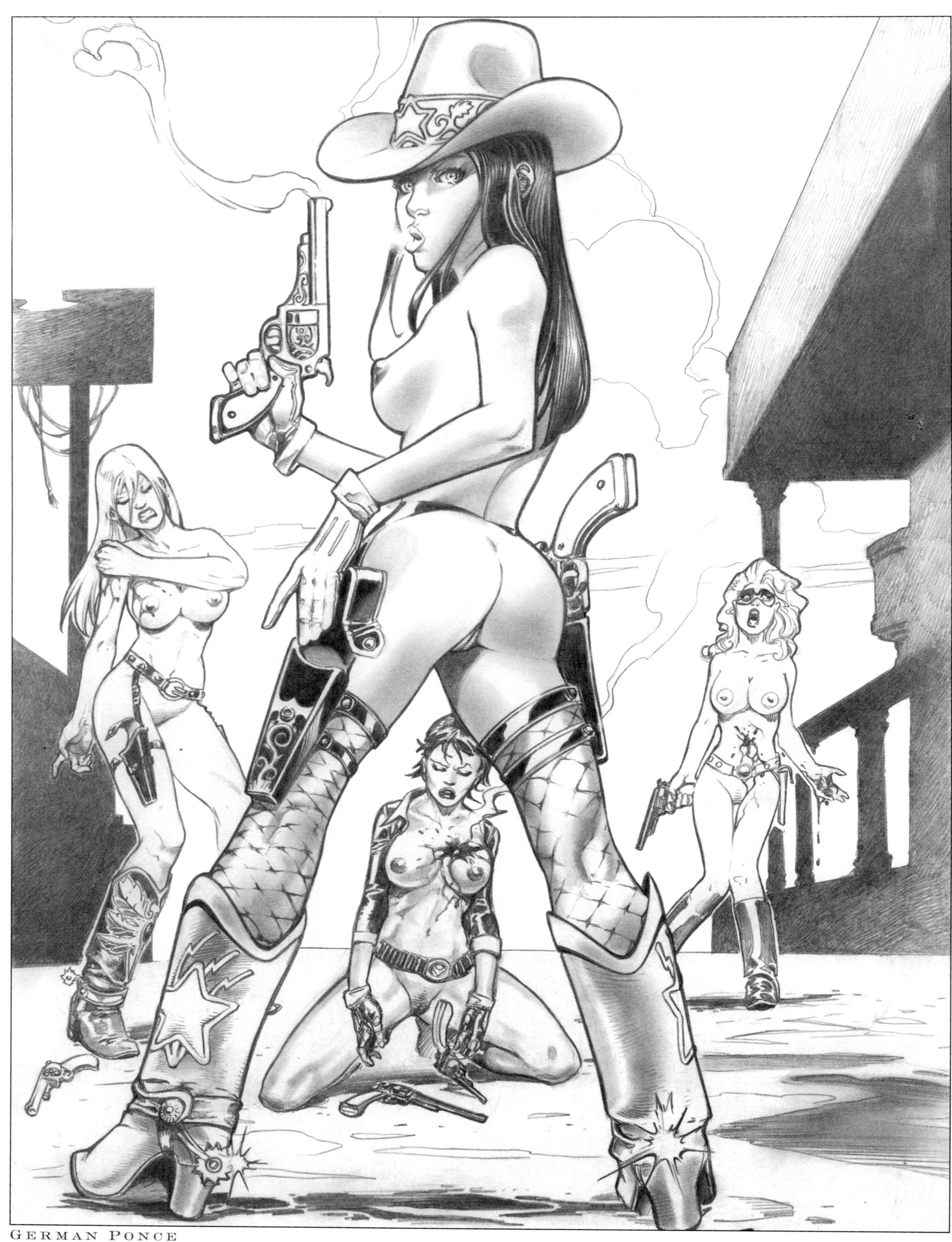

German Ponce

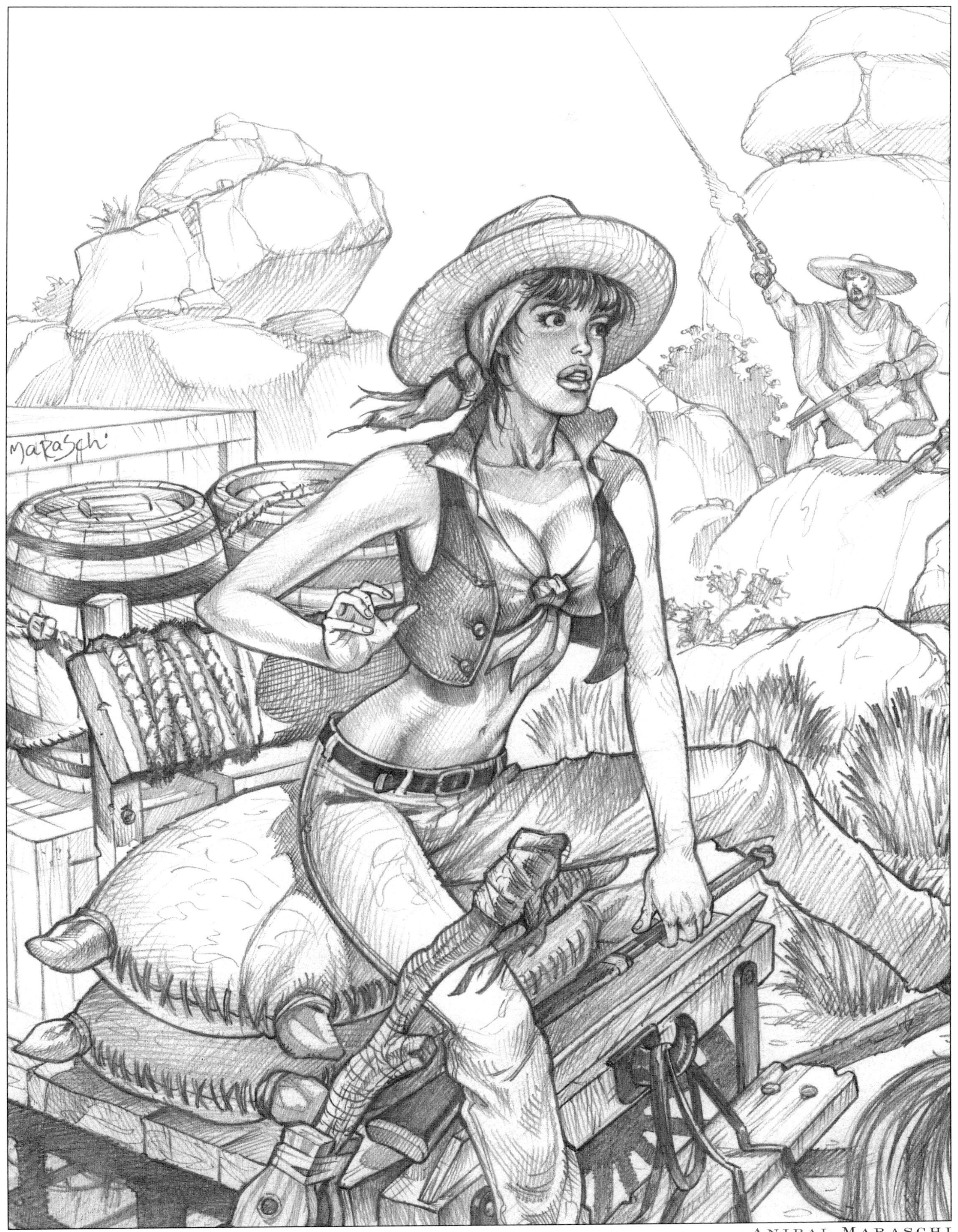

ANIBAL MARASCHI

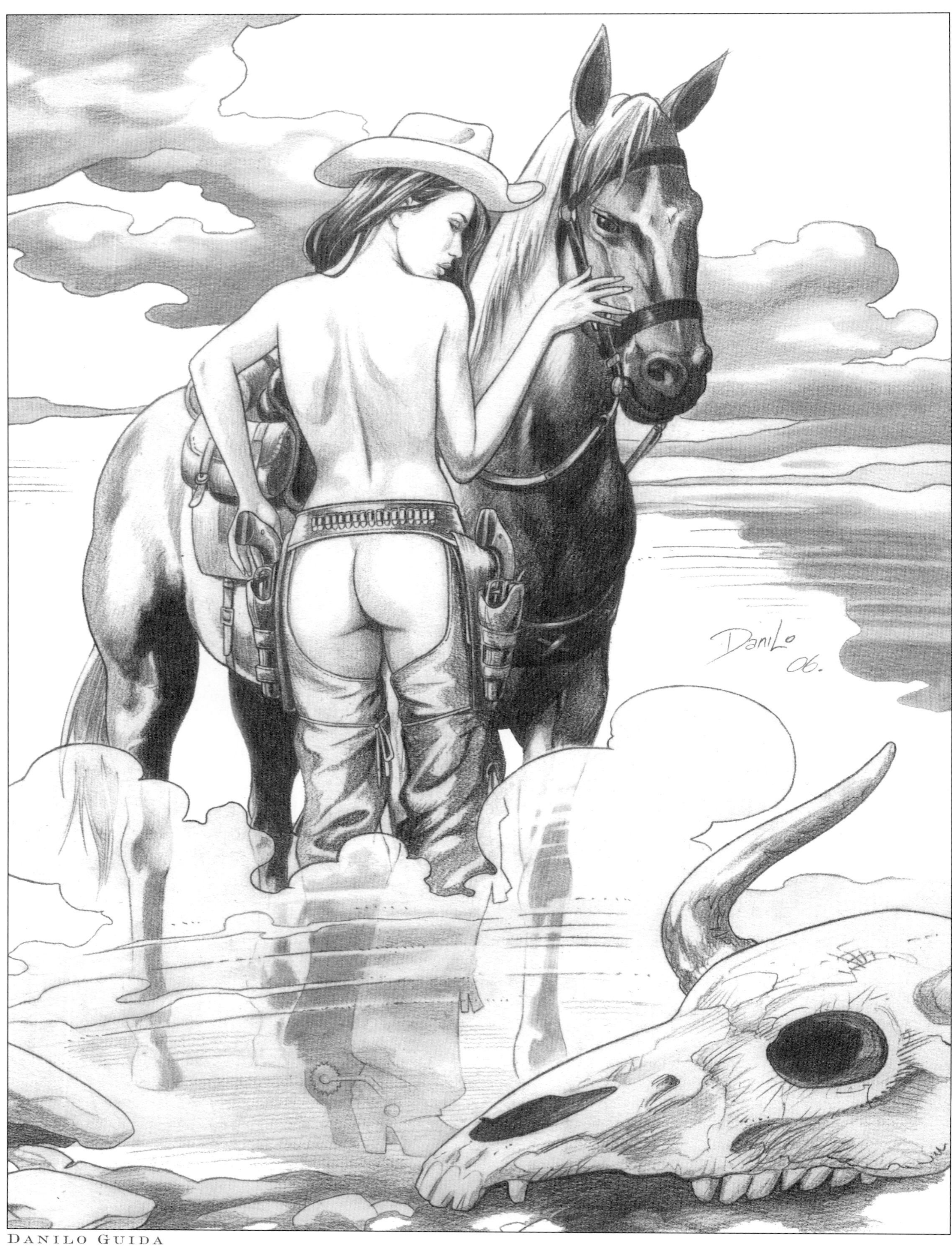

DANILO GUIDA

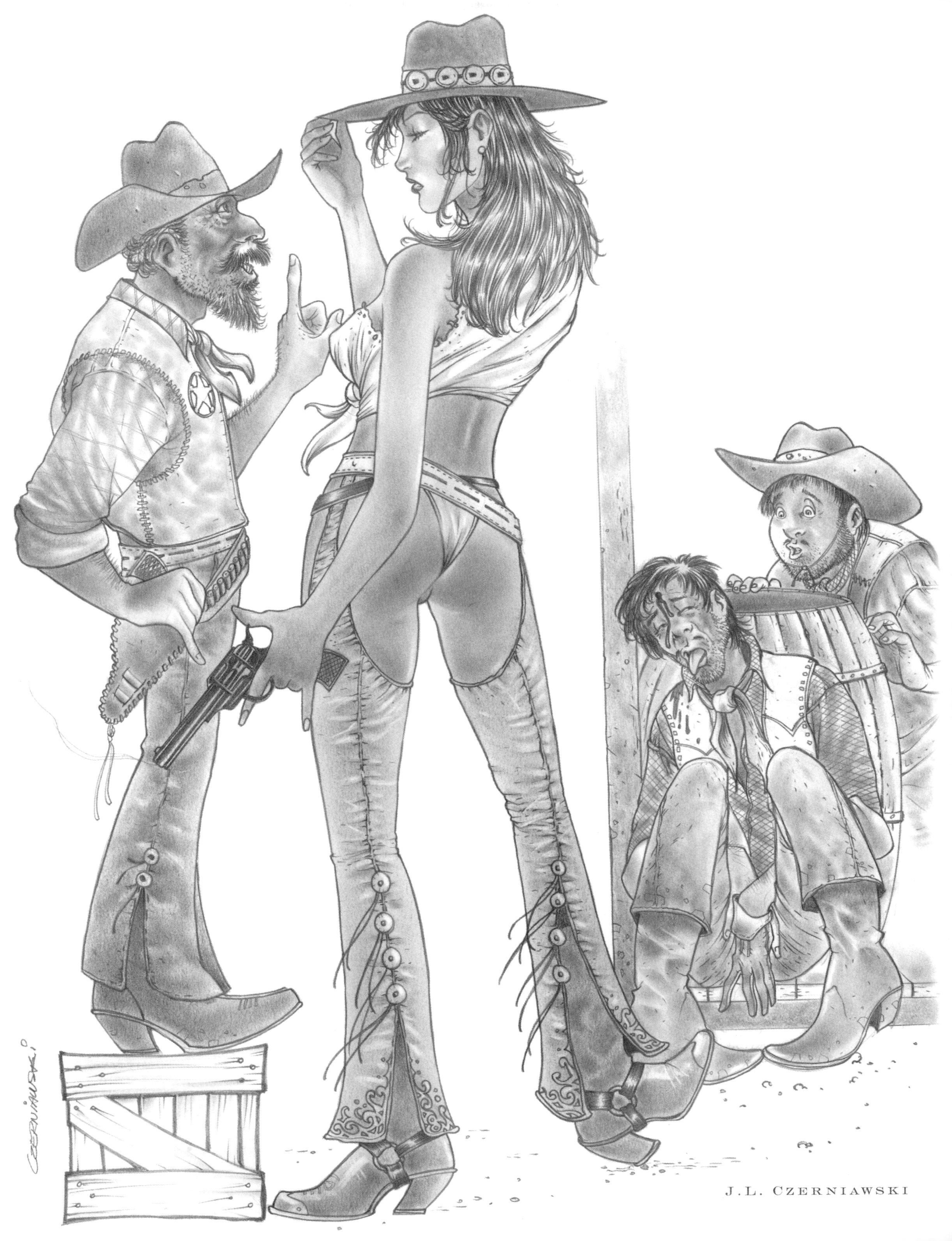

J.L. CZERNIAWSKI

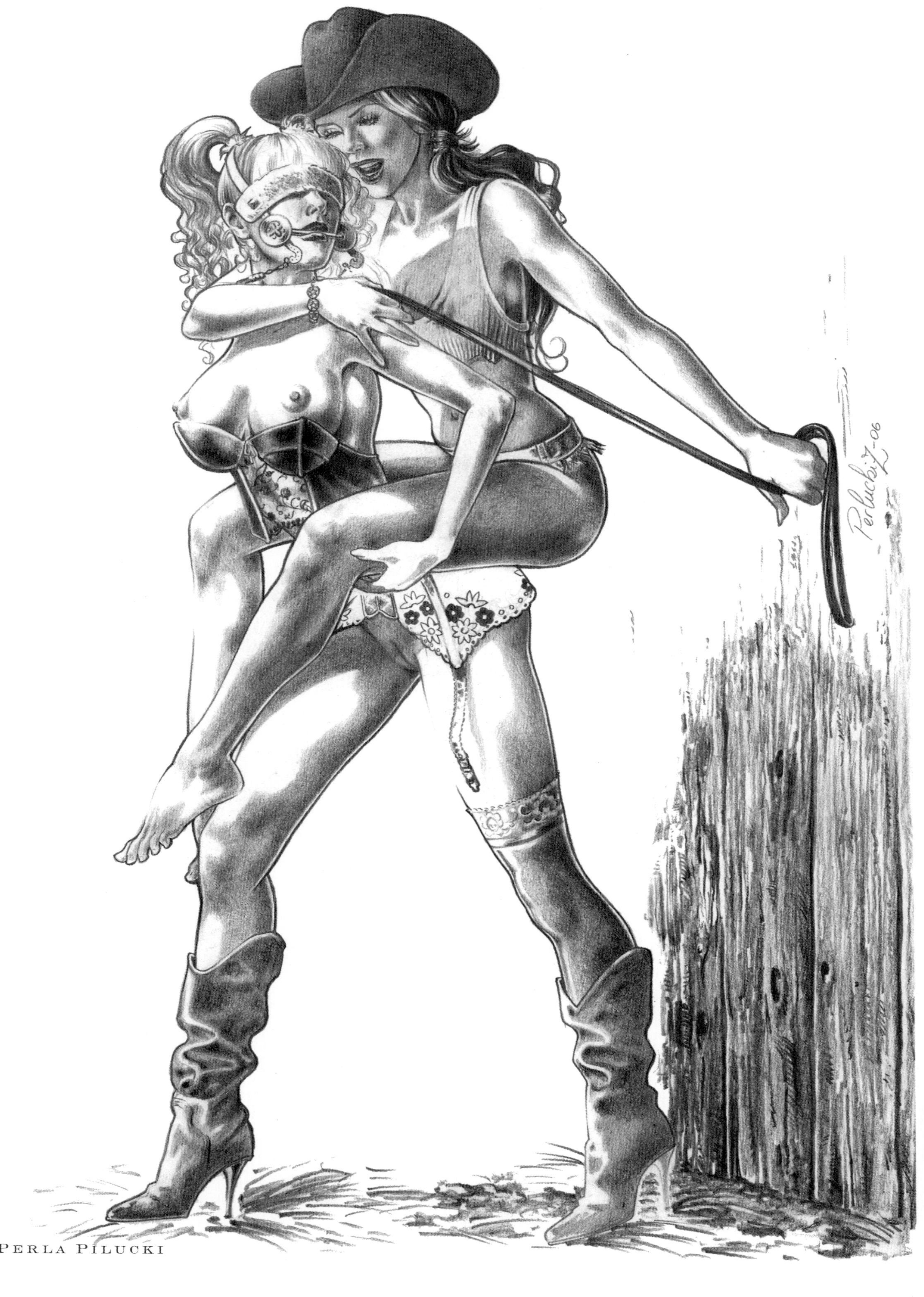

Perla Pilucki

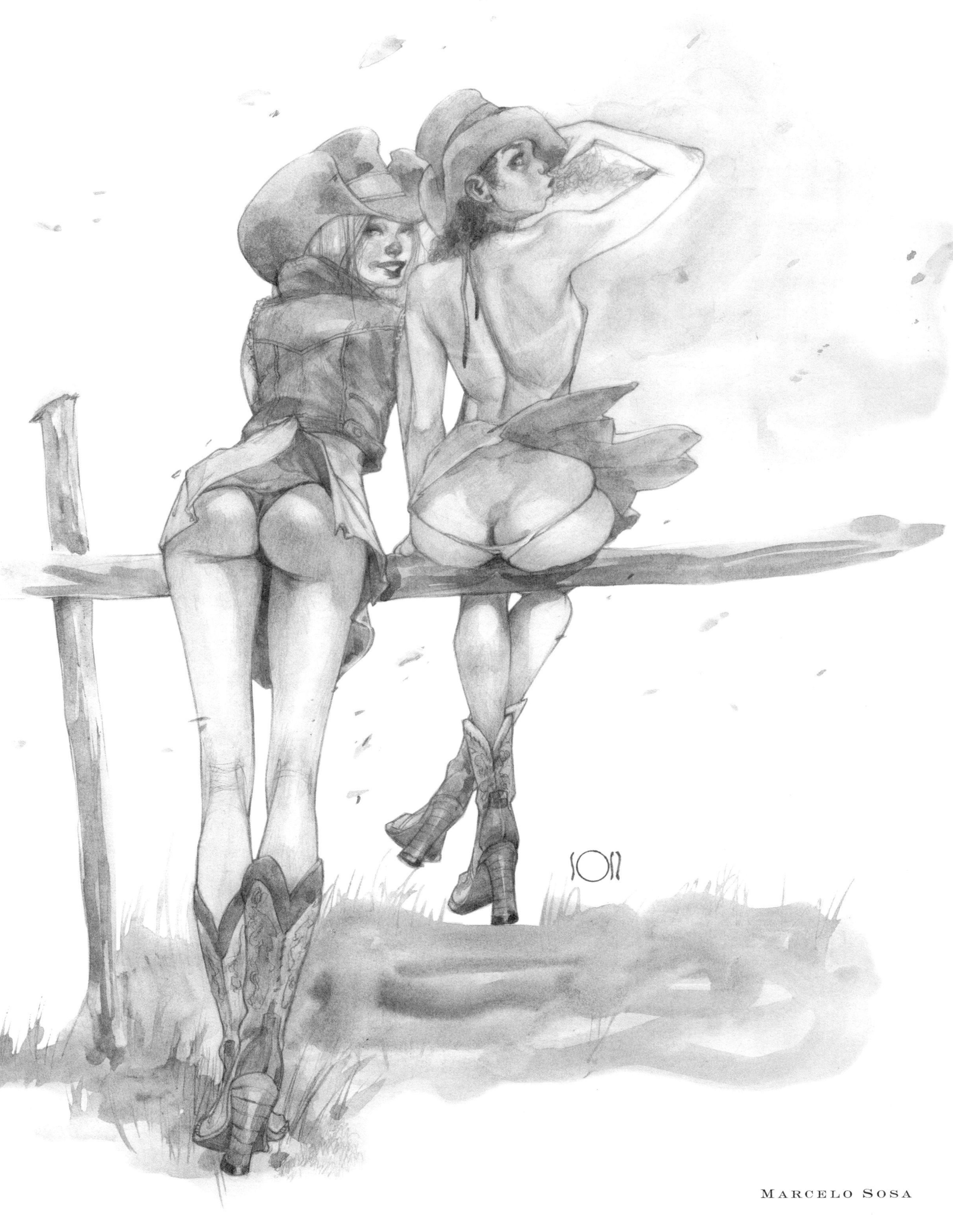

Marcelo Sosa

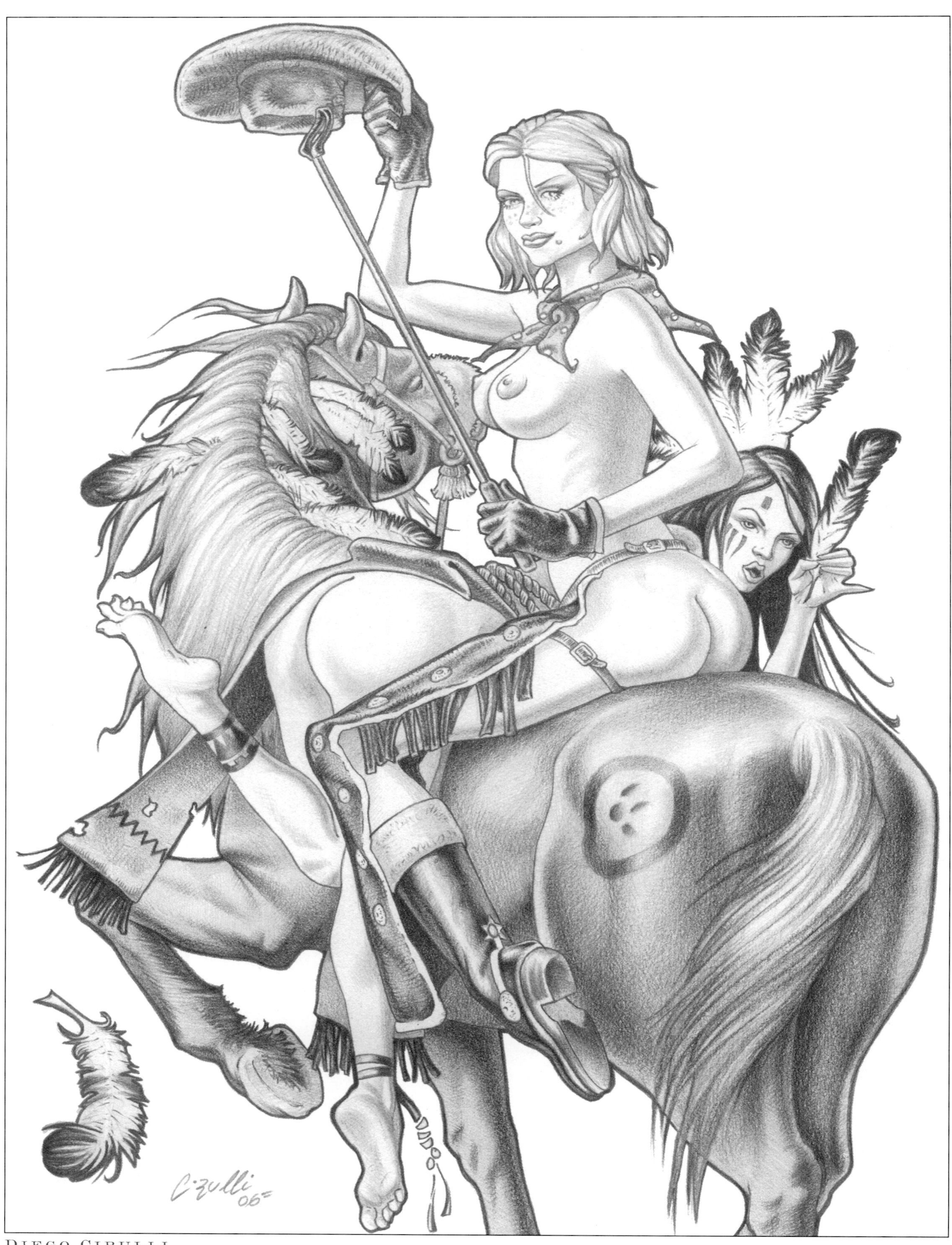

Diego Cirulli

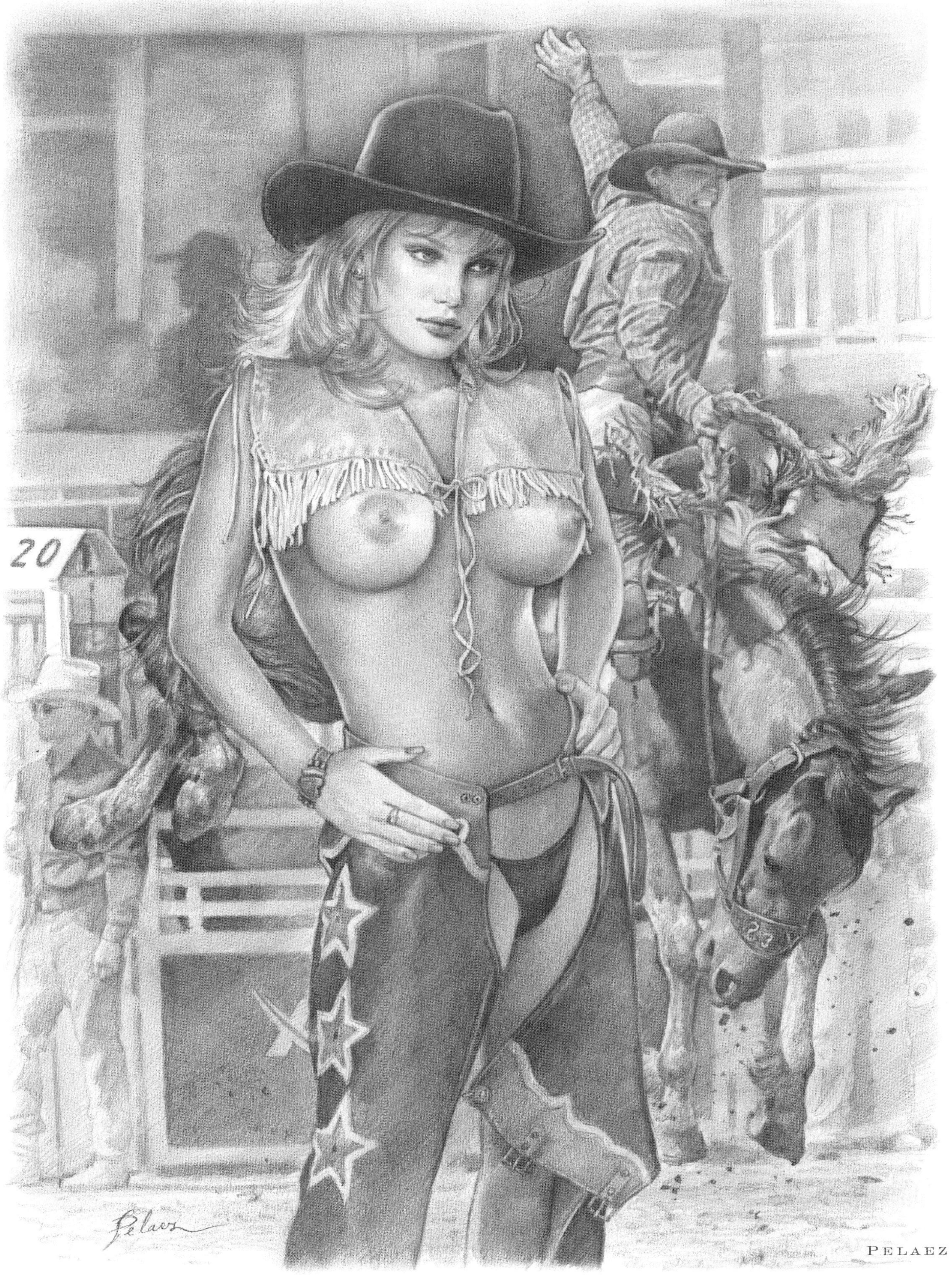

PELAEZ

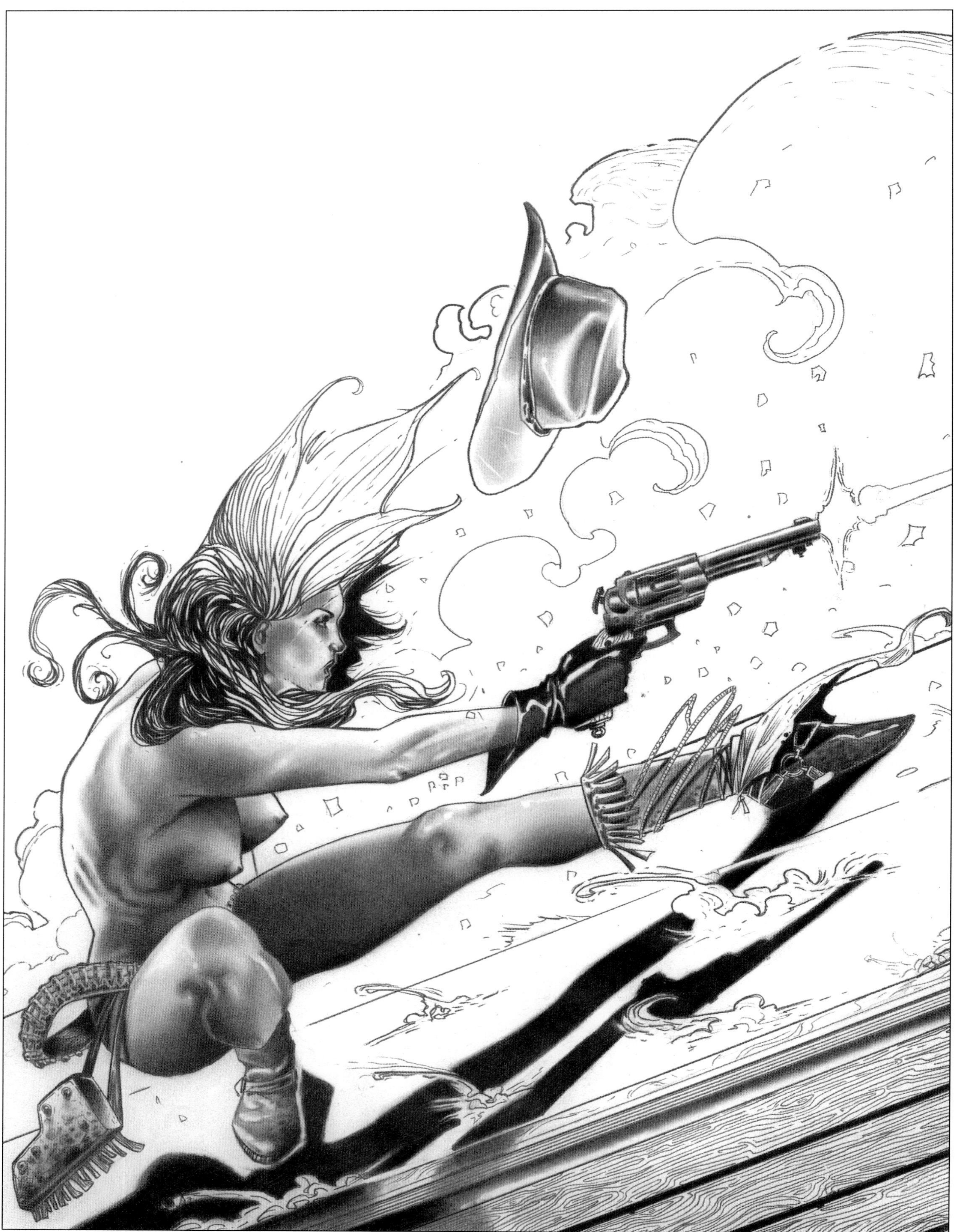

LUIS BUCI

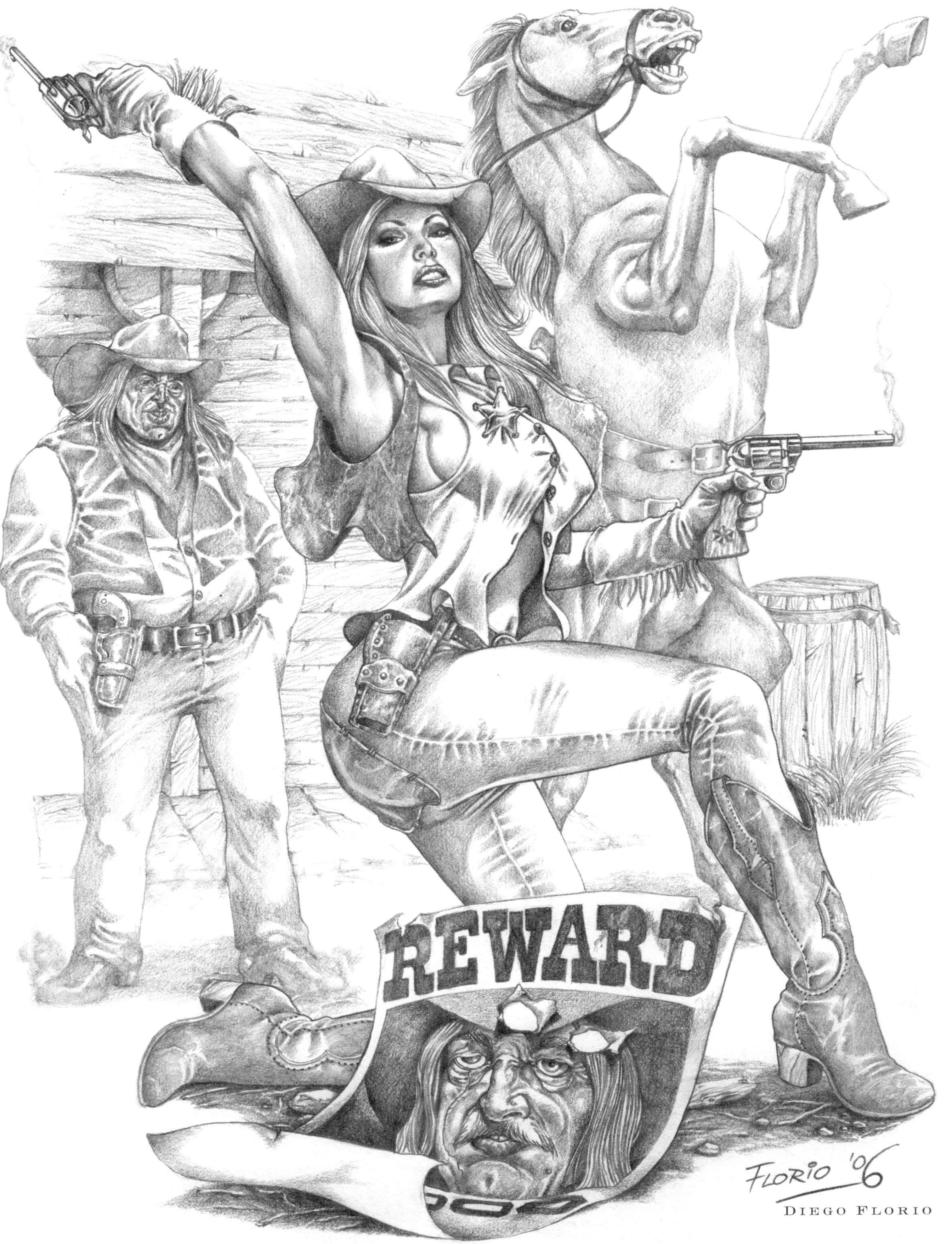

DIEGO FLORIO

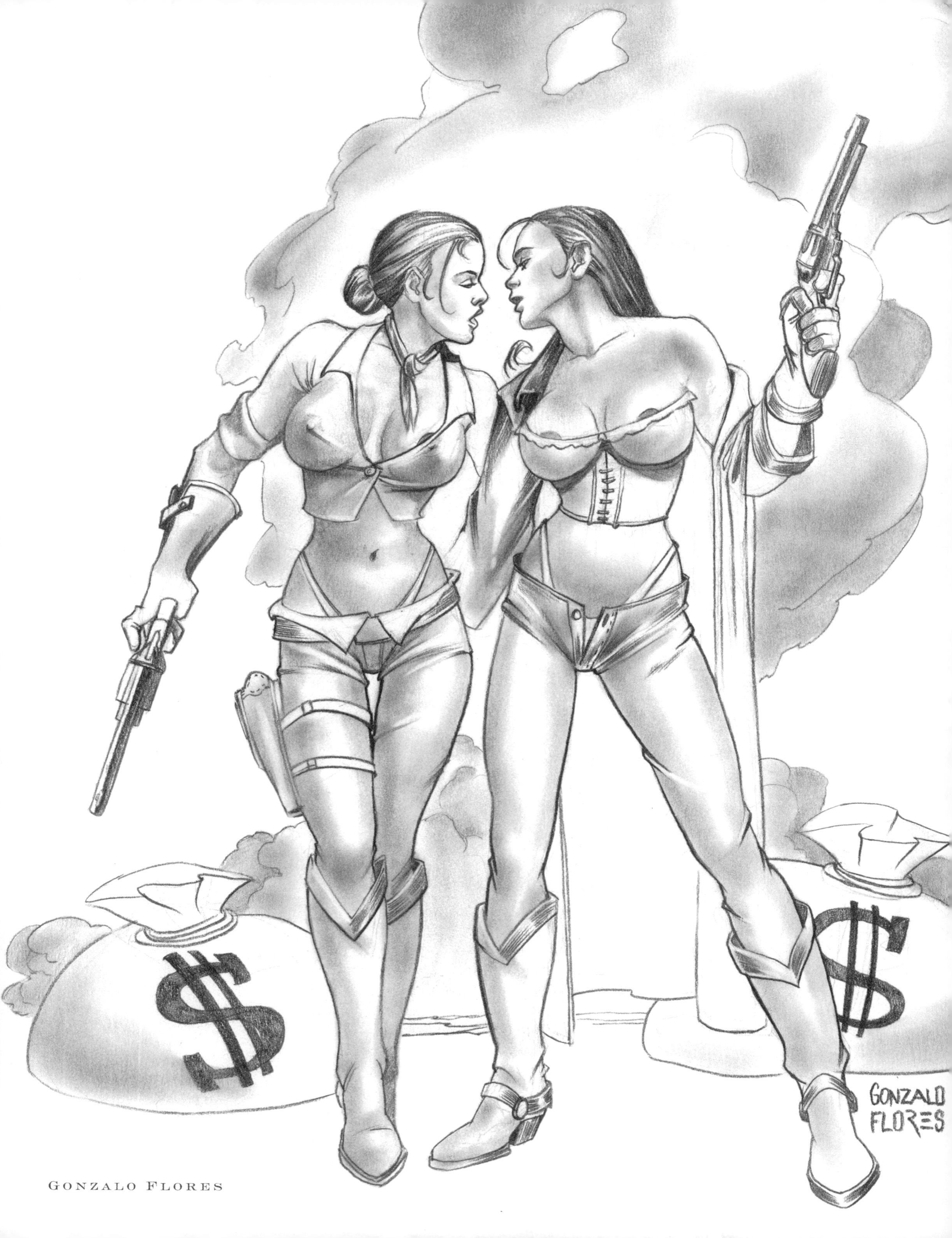

GONZALO FLORES

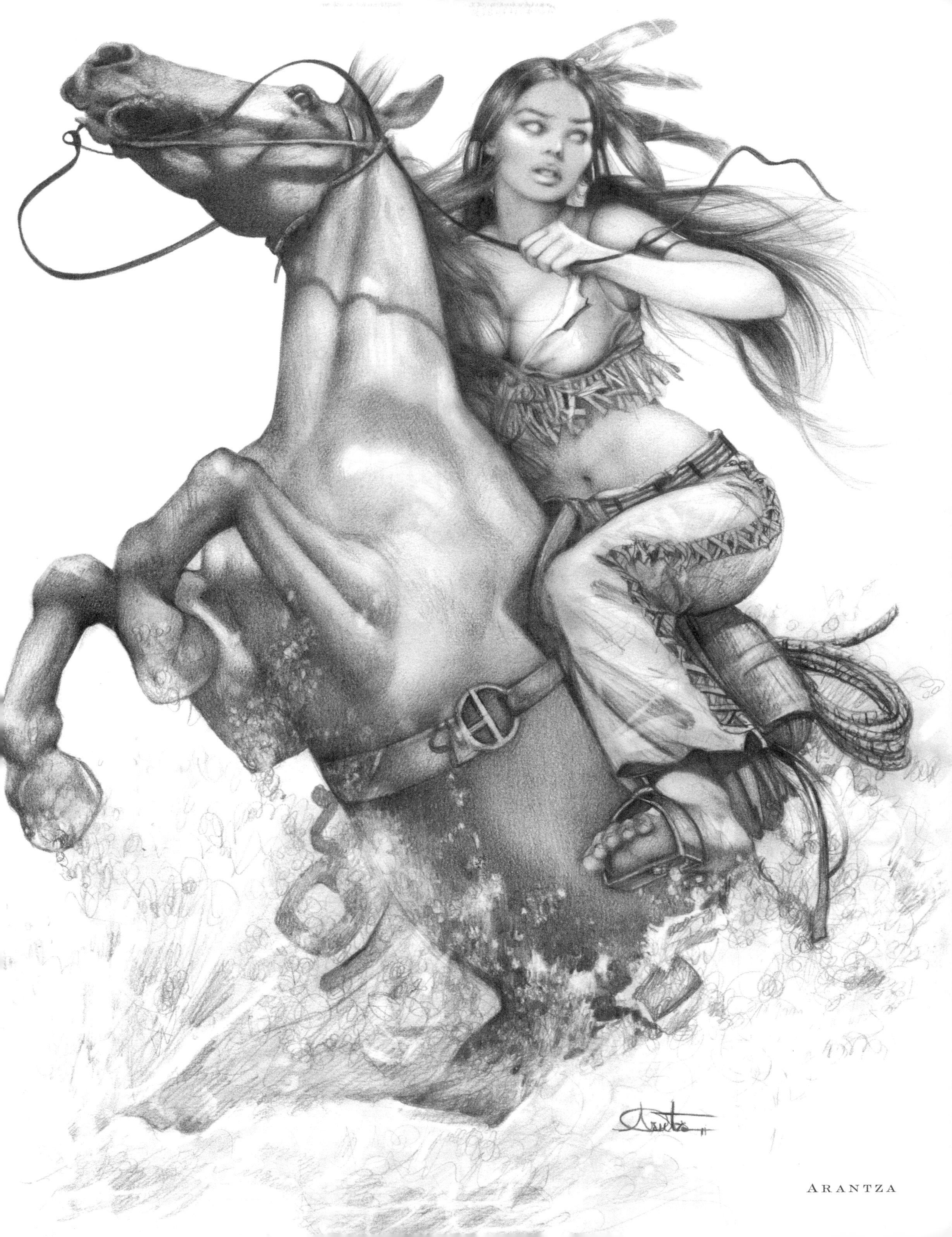

ARANTZA

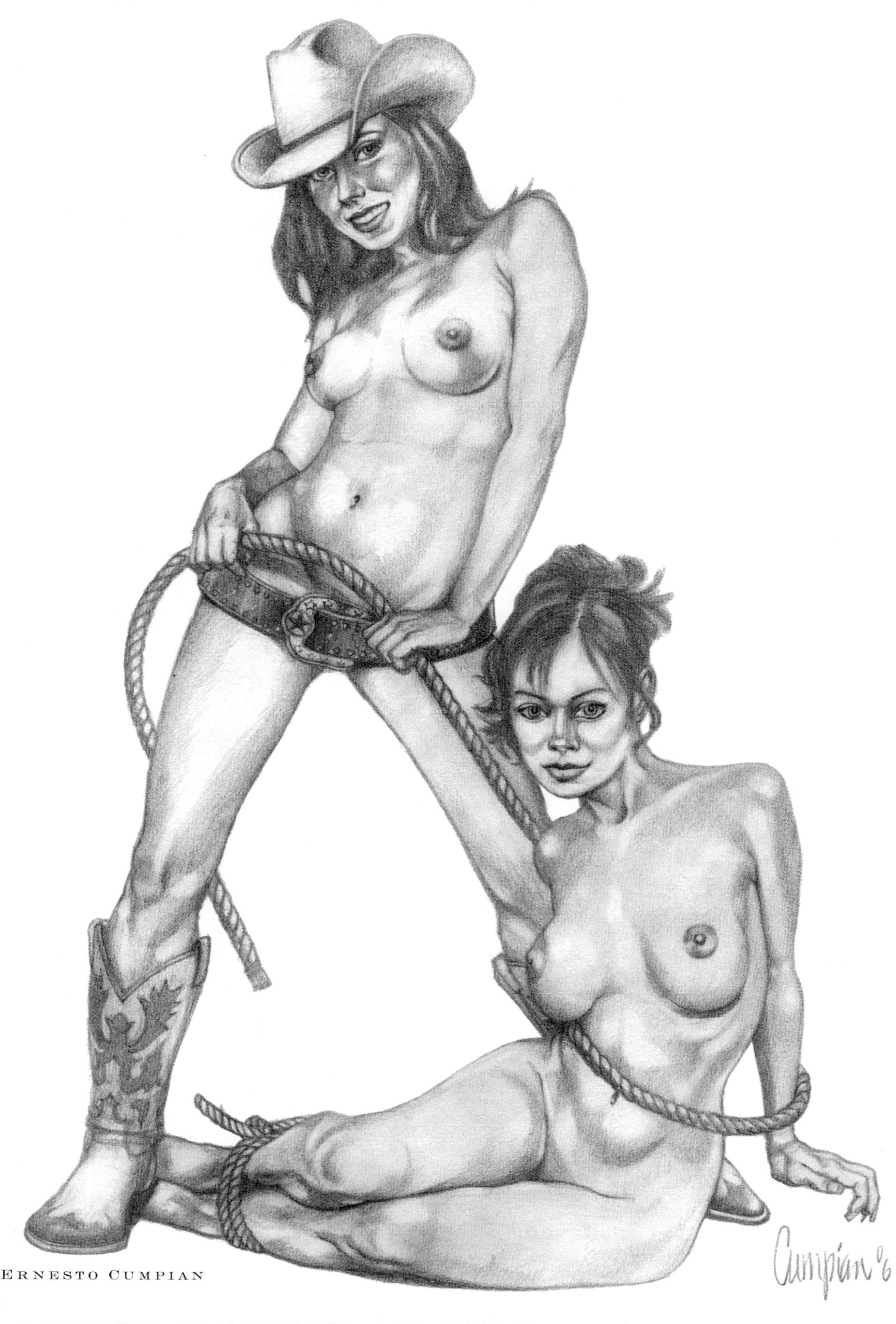

ERNESTO CUMPIAN

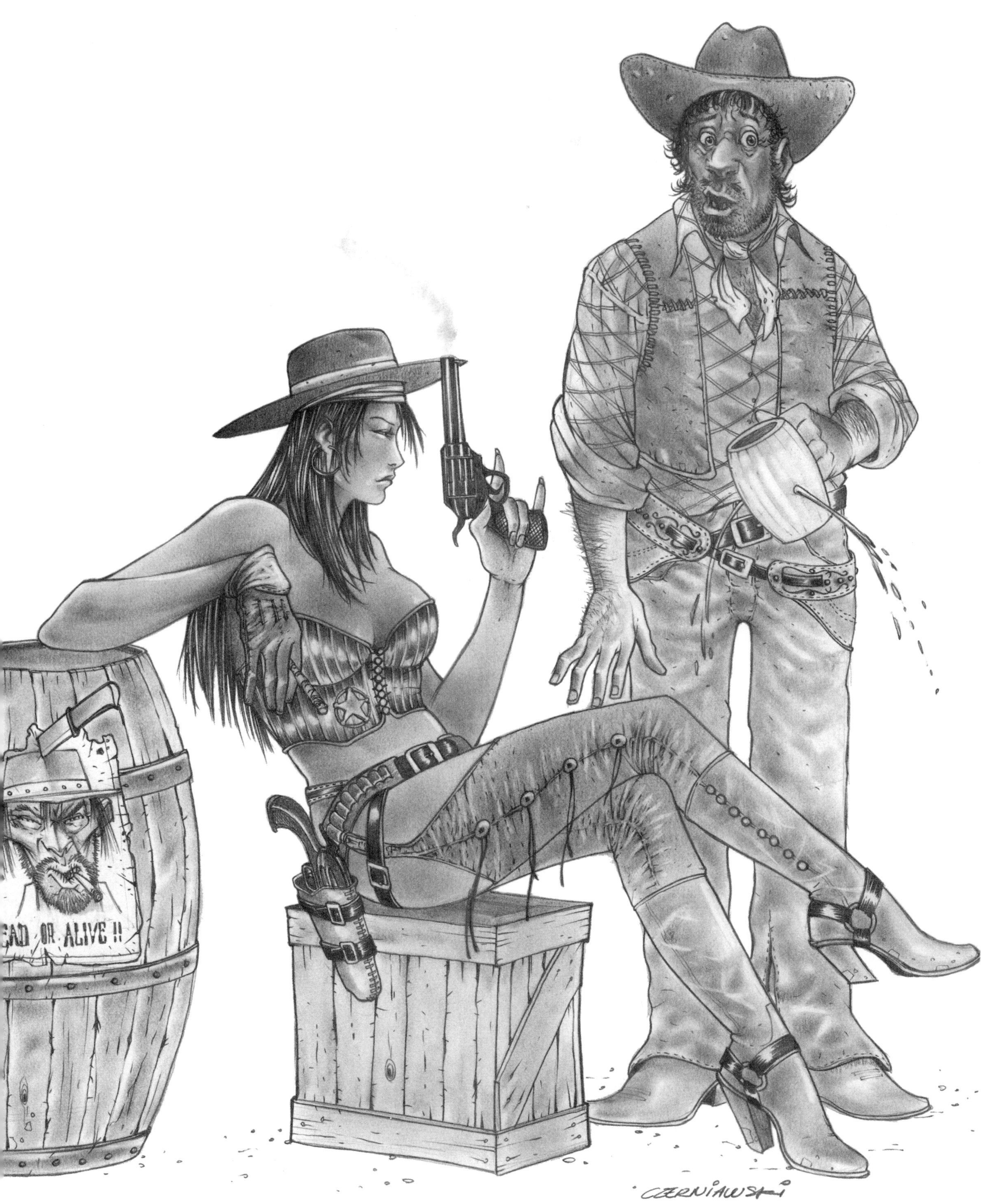

J.L. CZERNIAWSKI

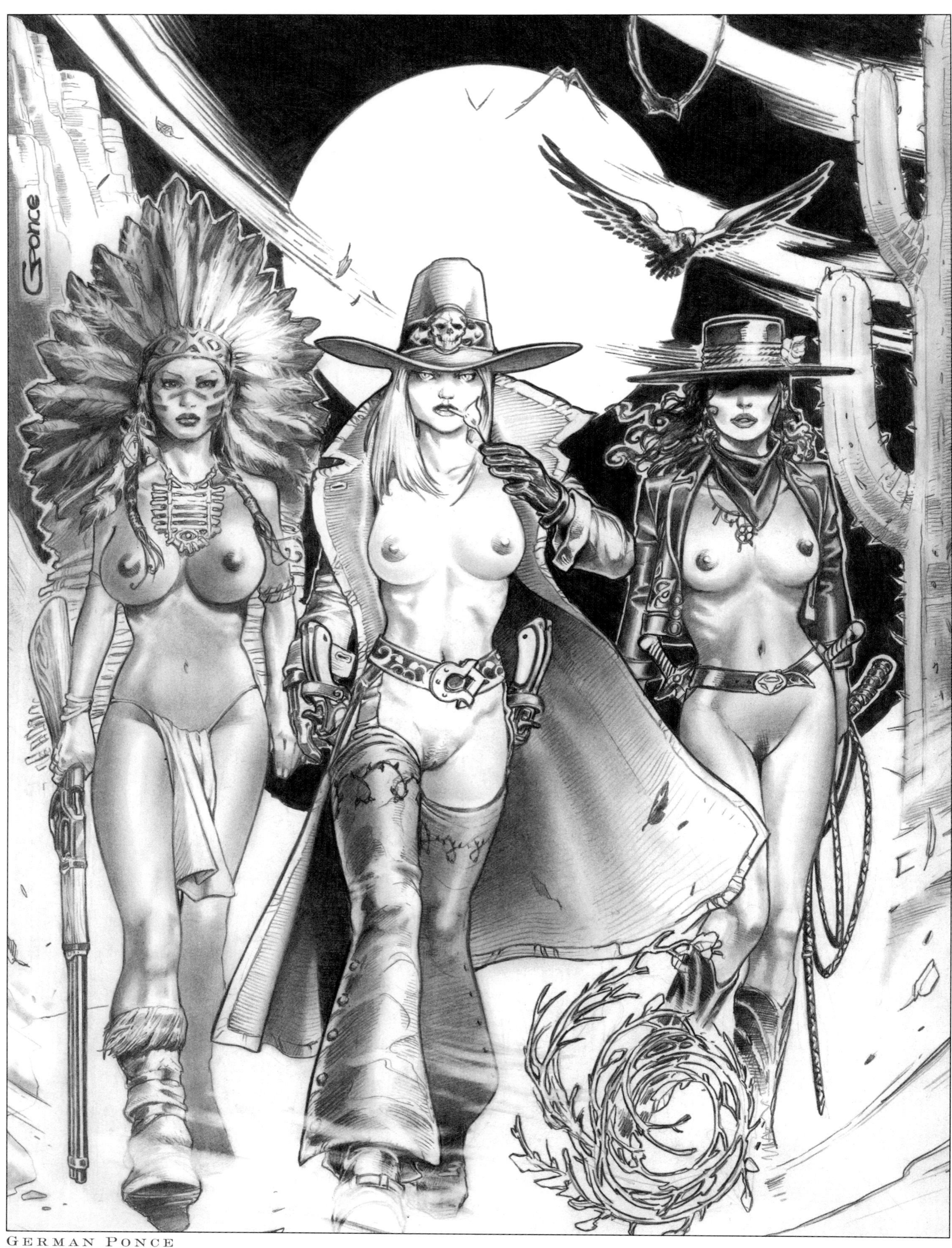

GERMAN PONCE

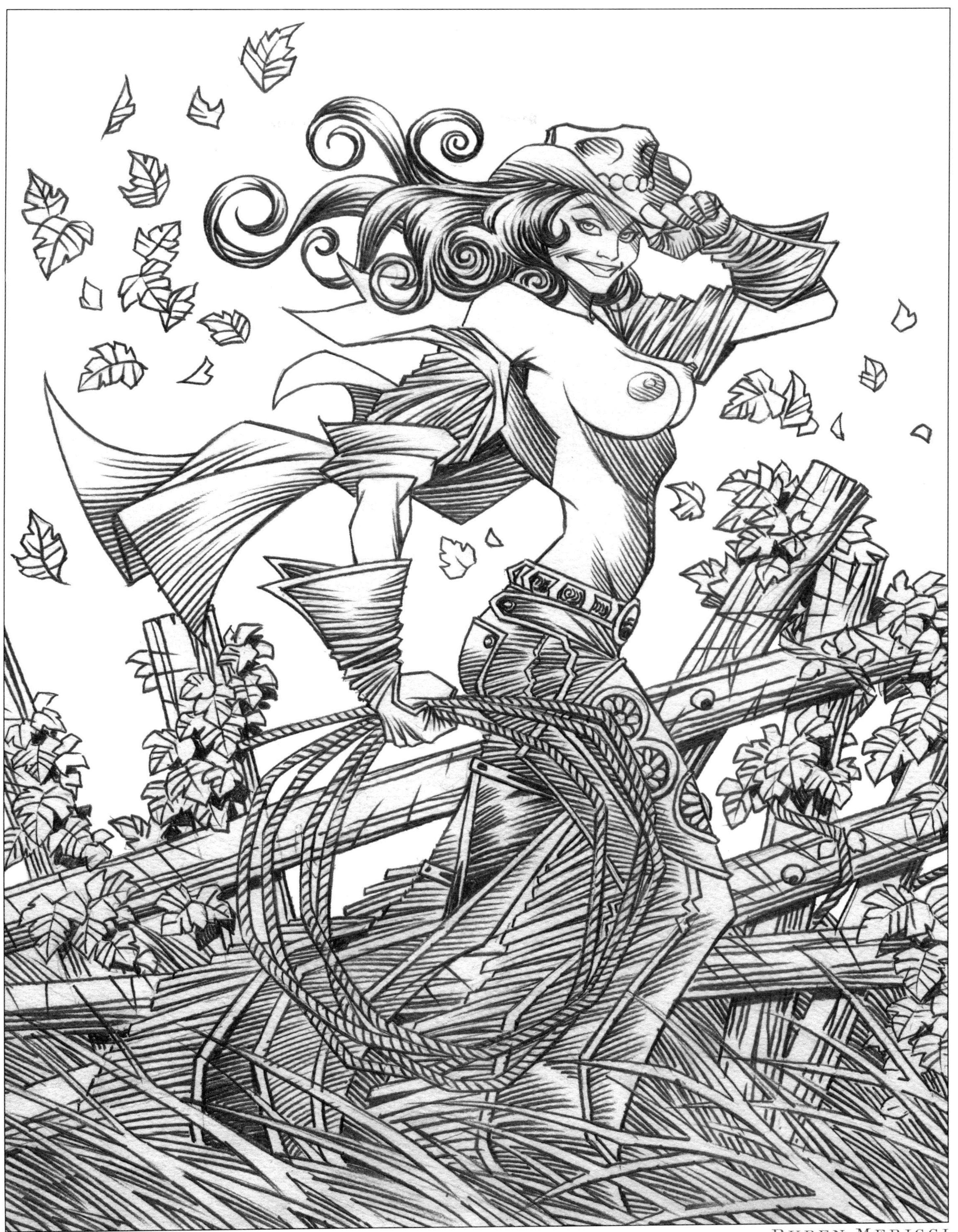

RUBEN MERIGGI

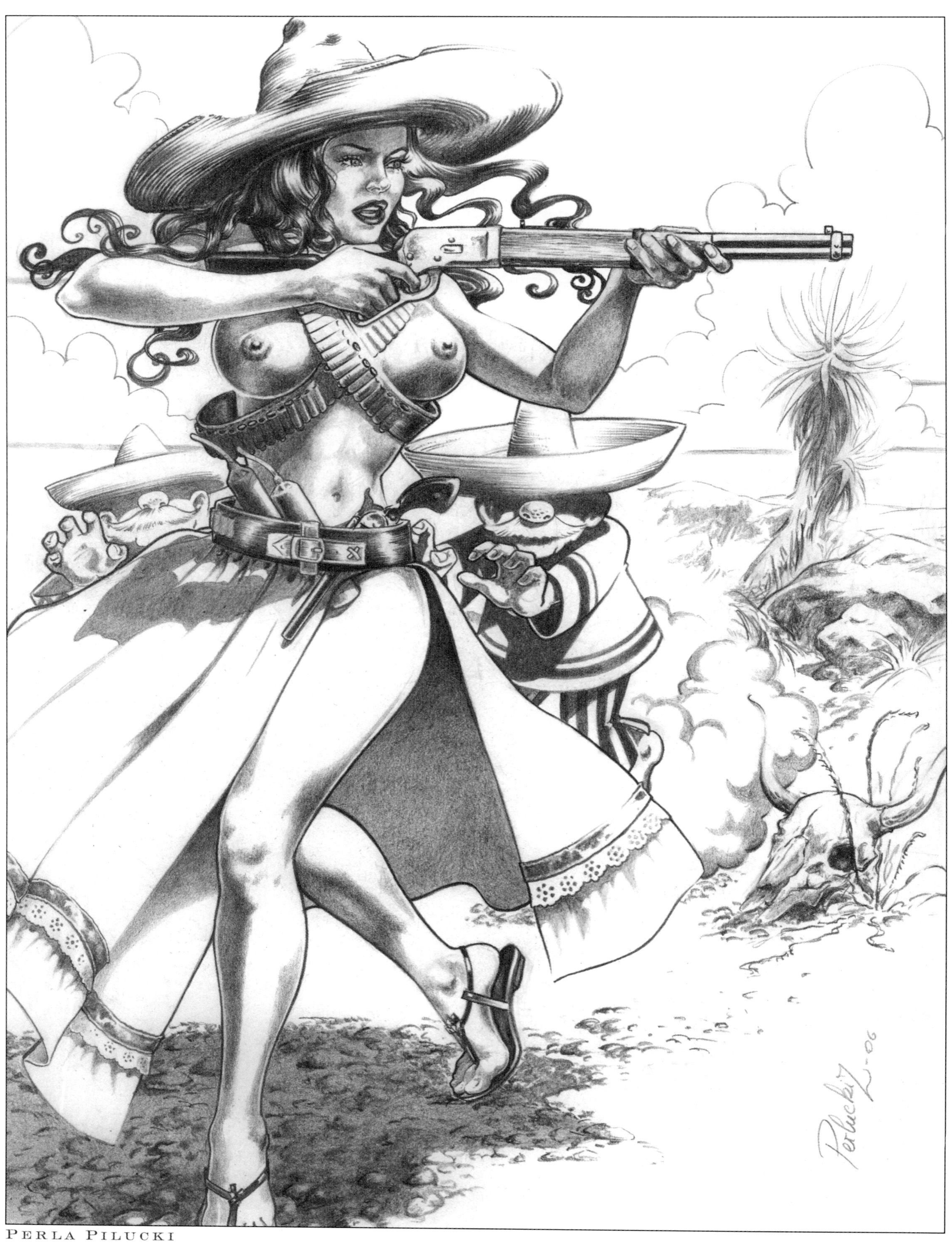

PERLA PILUCKI

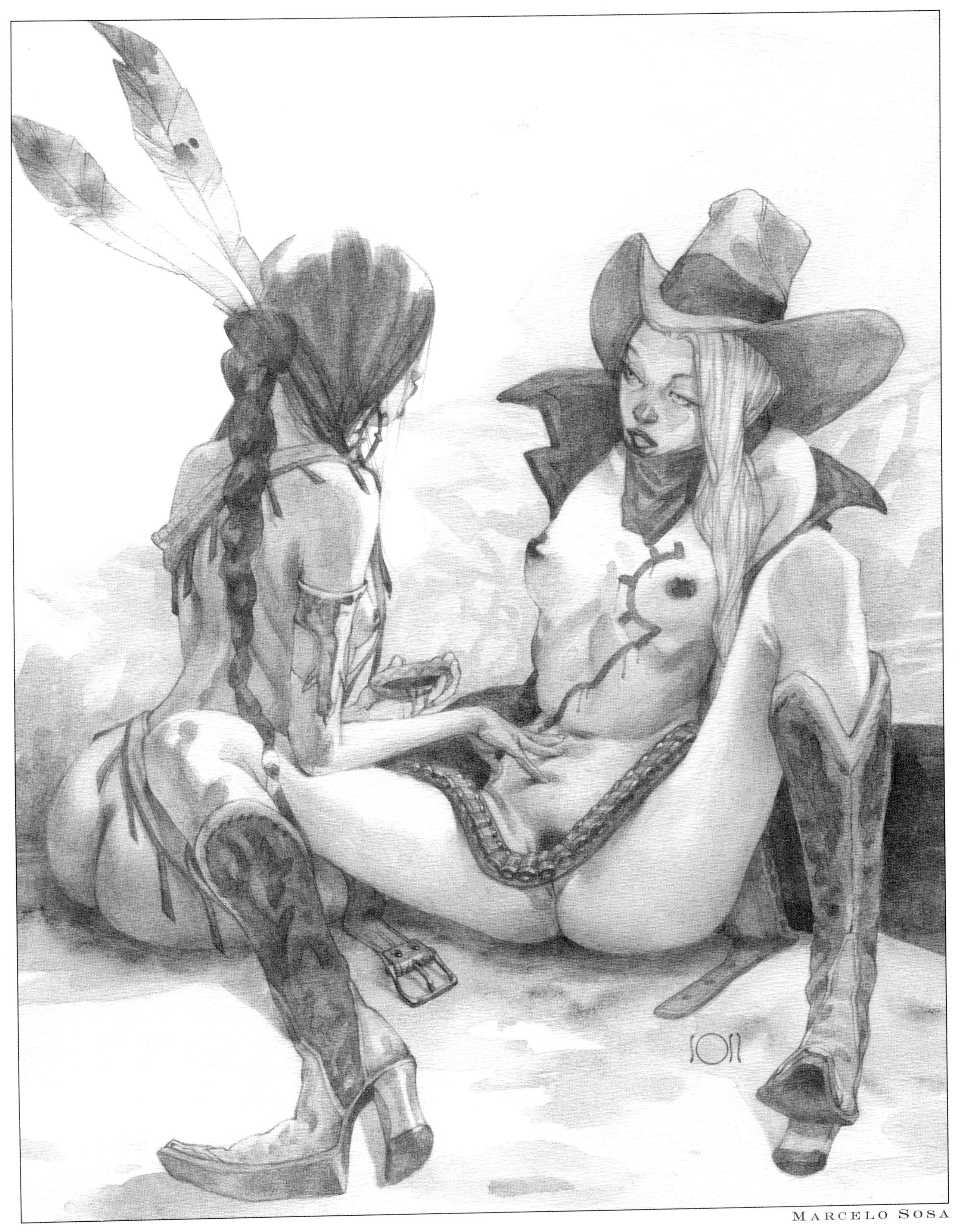

Marcelo Sosa

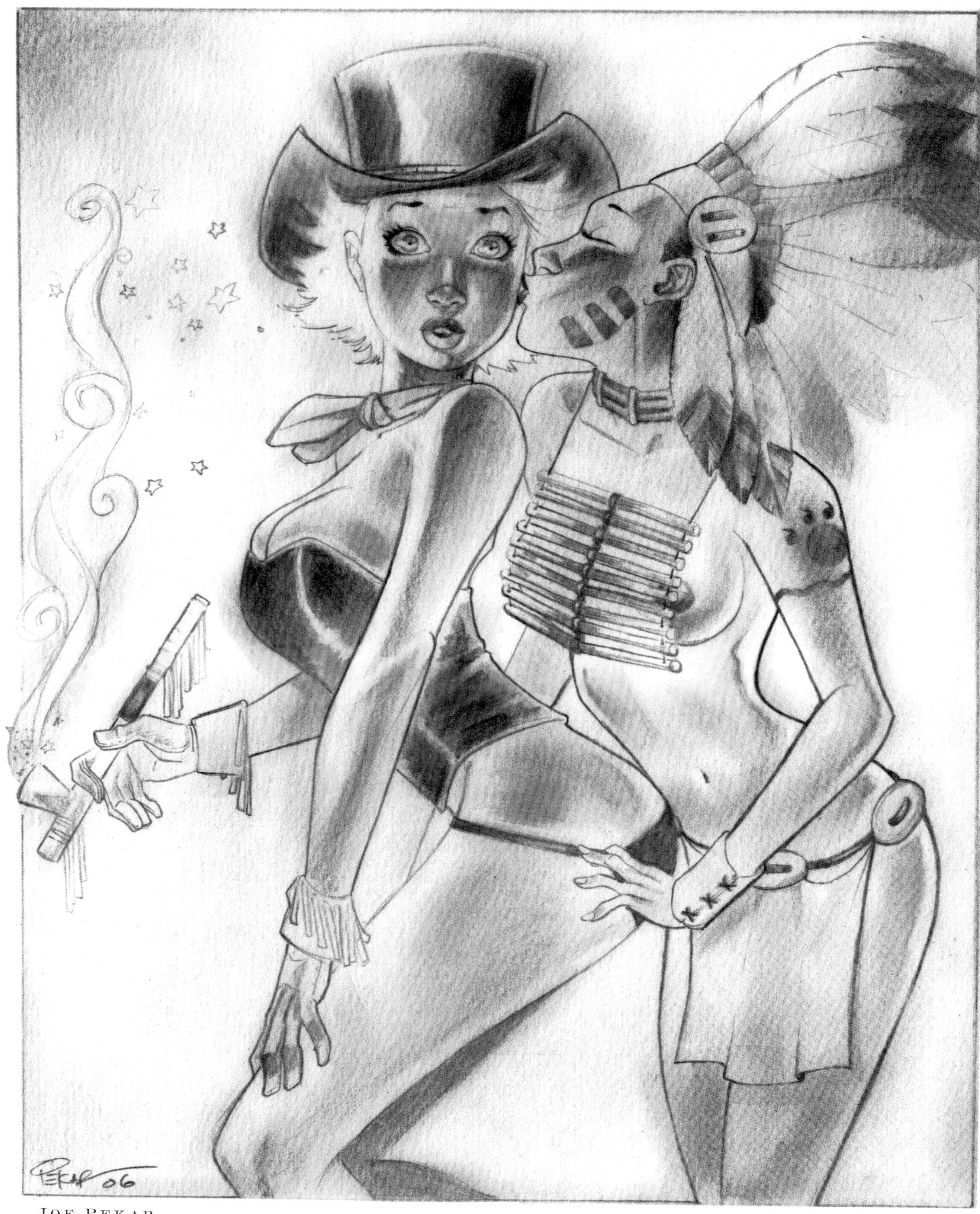

JOE PEKAR

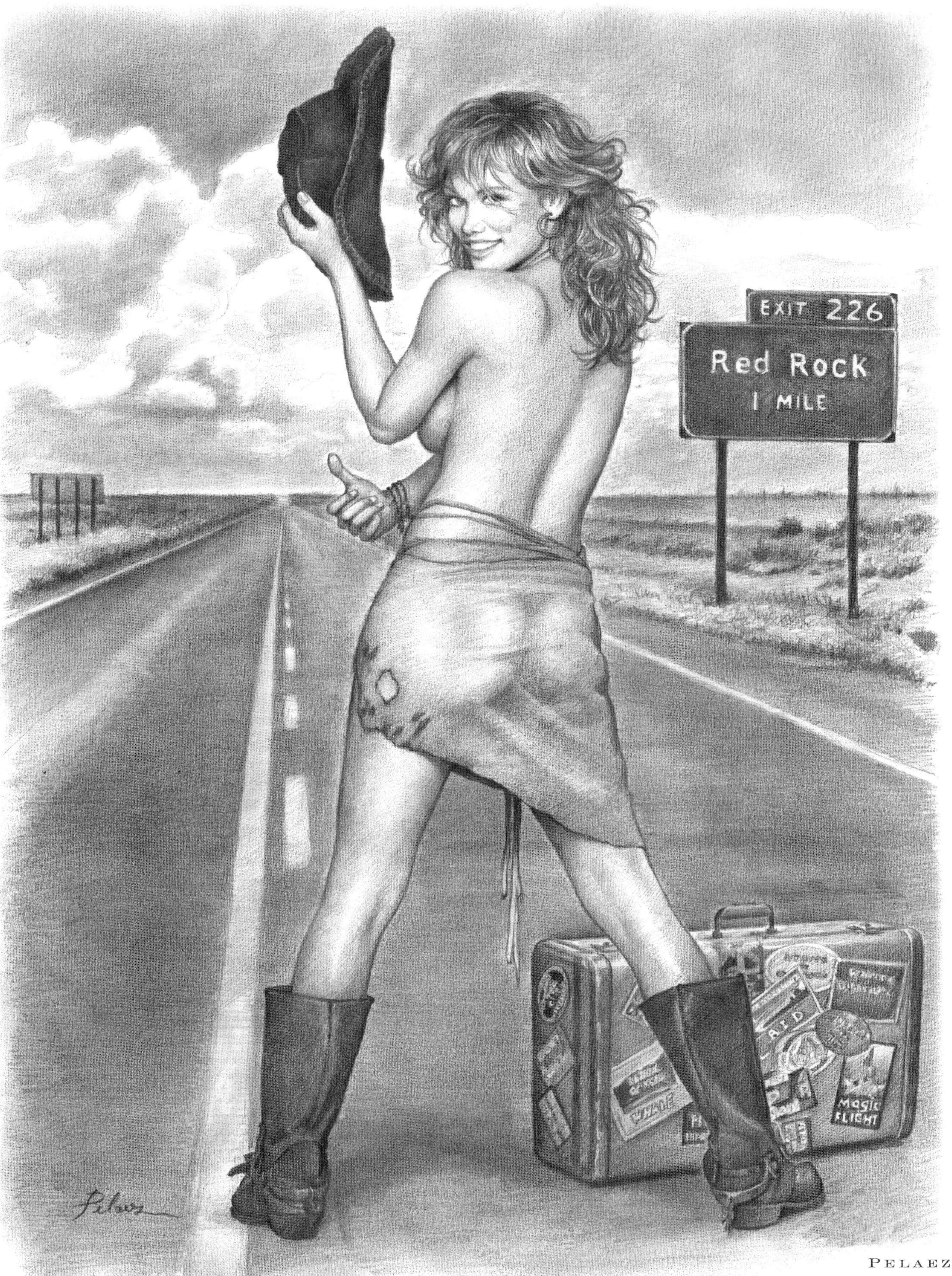

PELAEZ

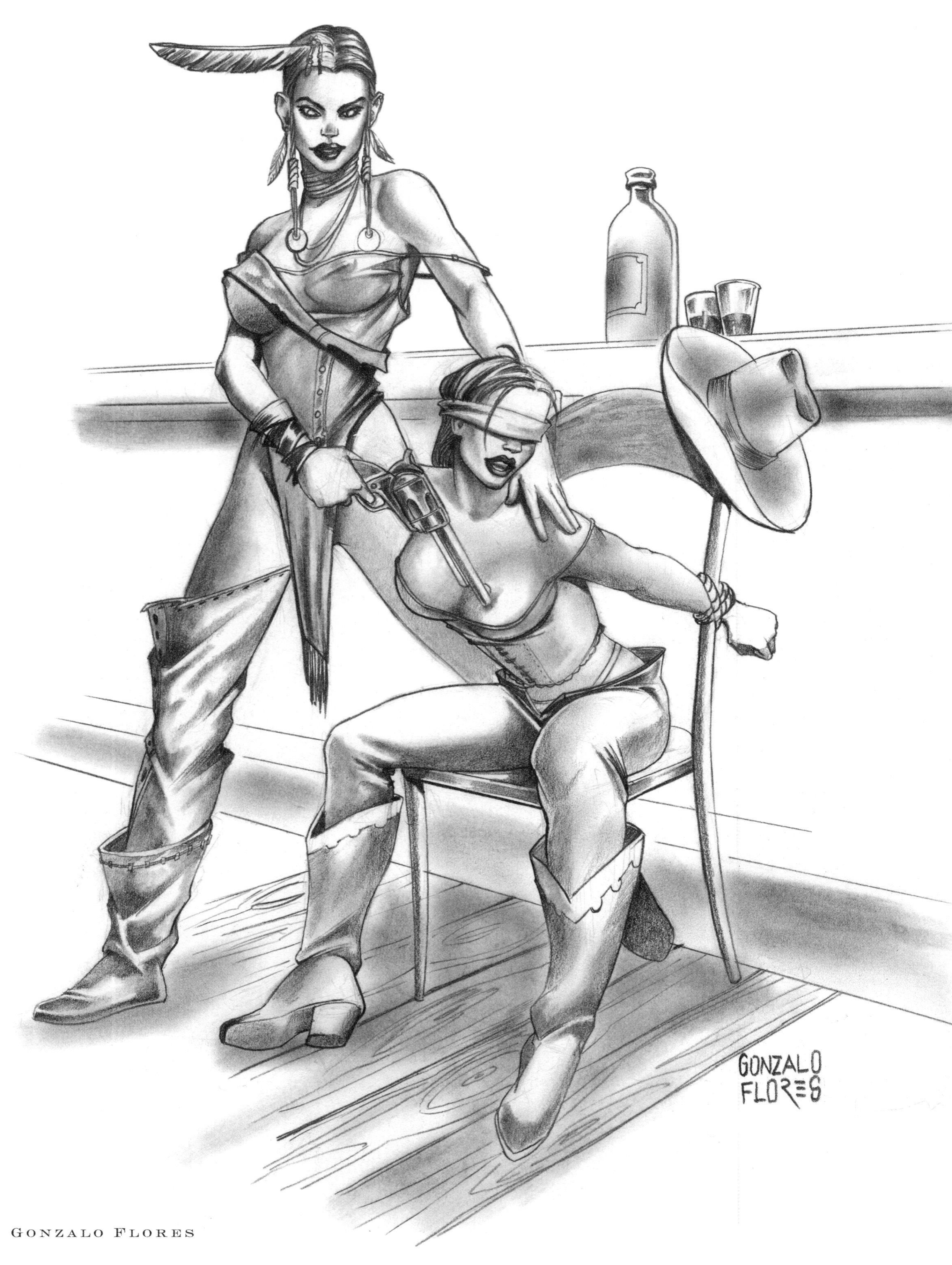

Gonzalo Flores

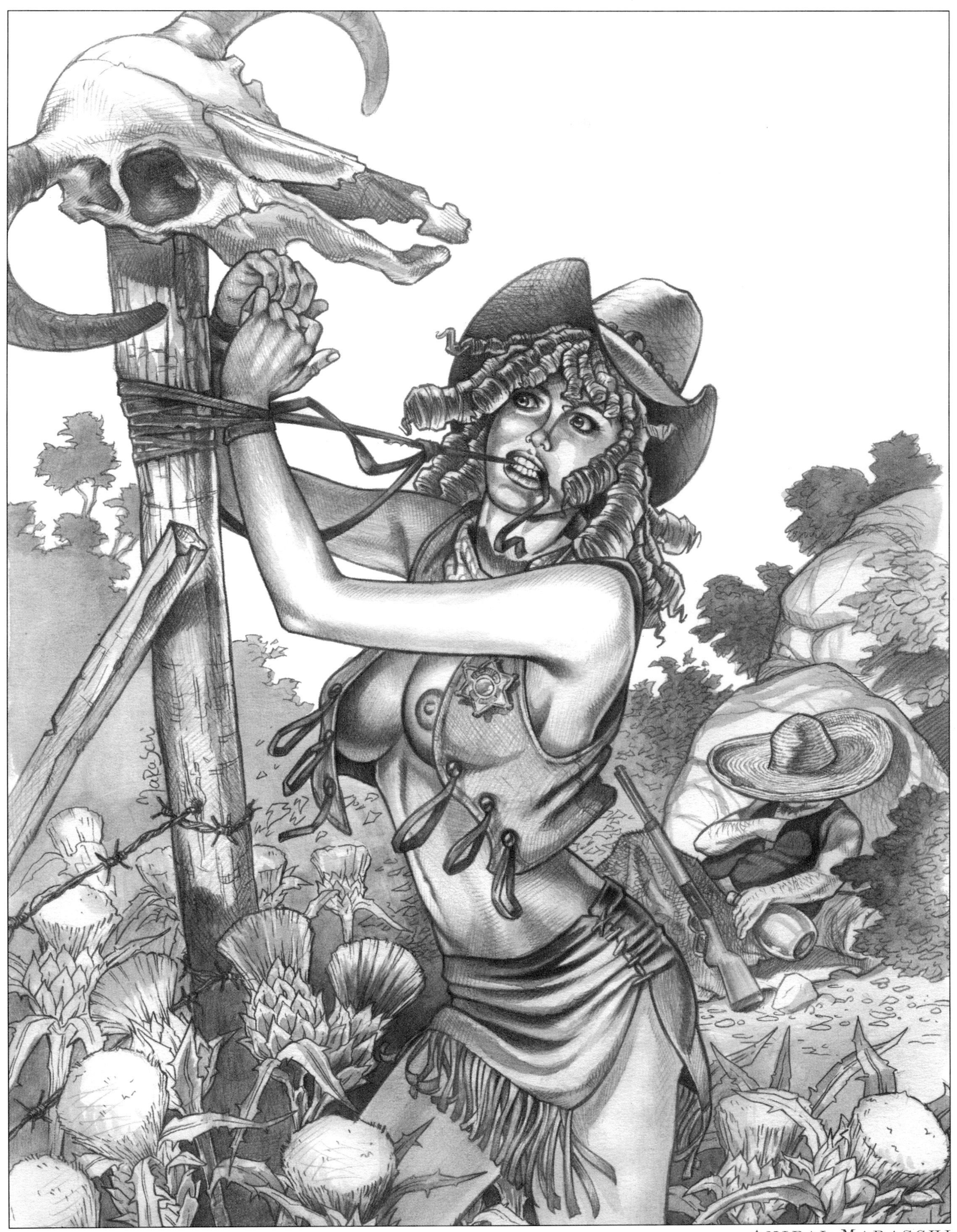

Anibal Maraschi

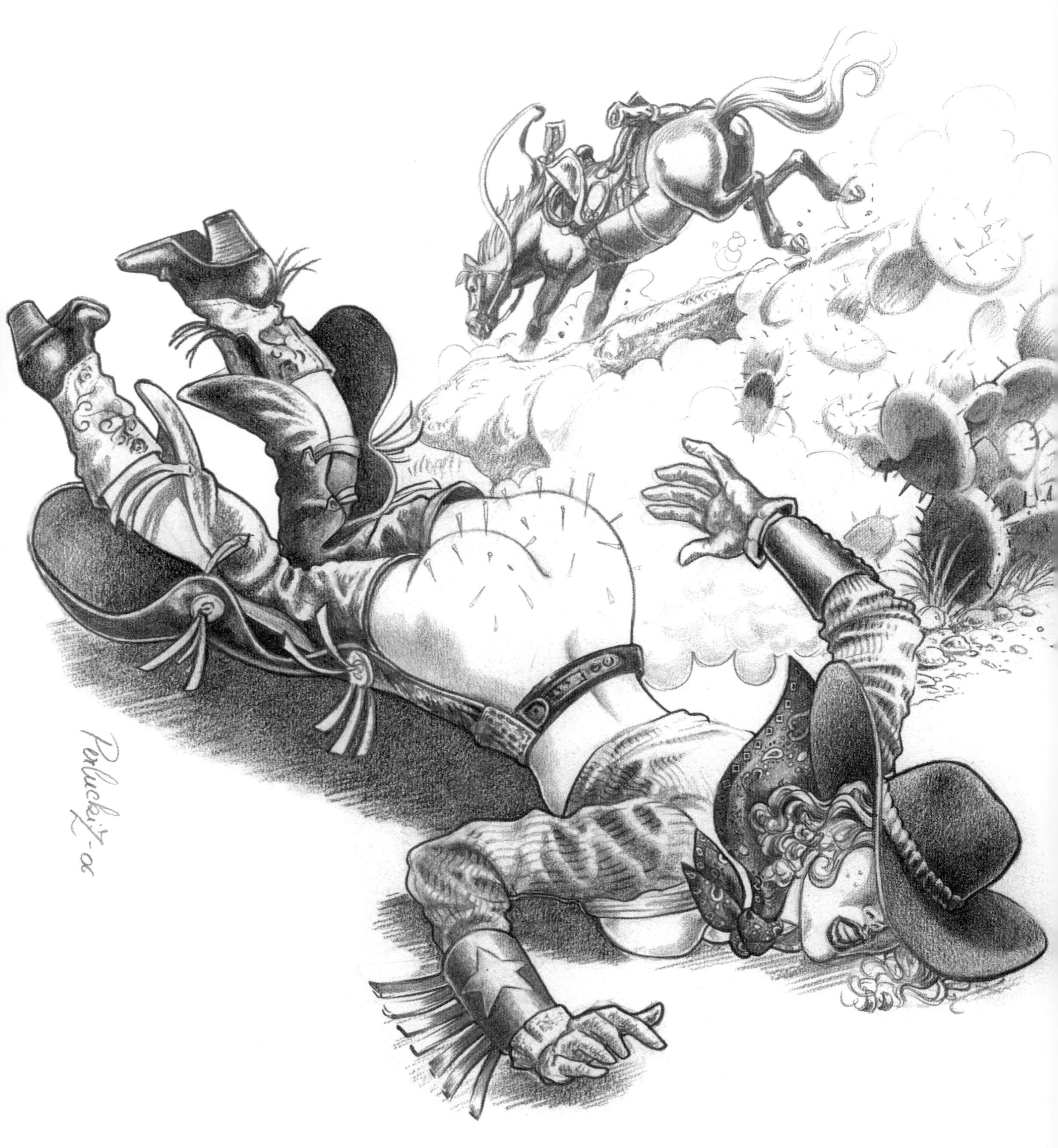

Perla Pilucki

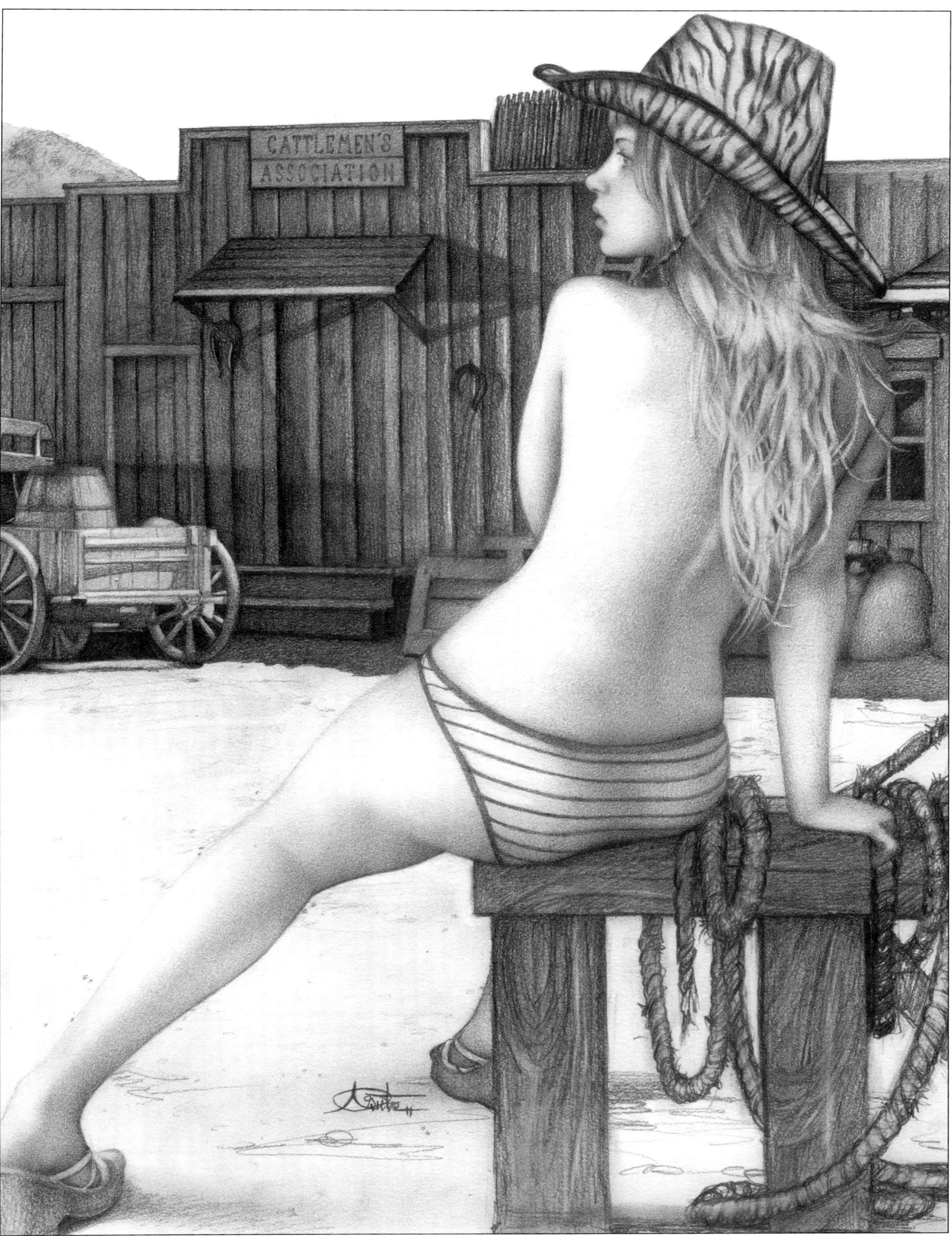

ARANTZA

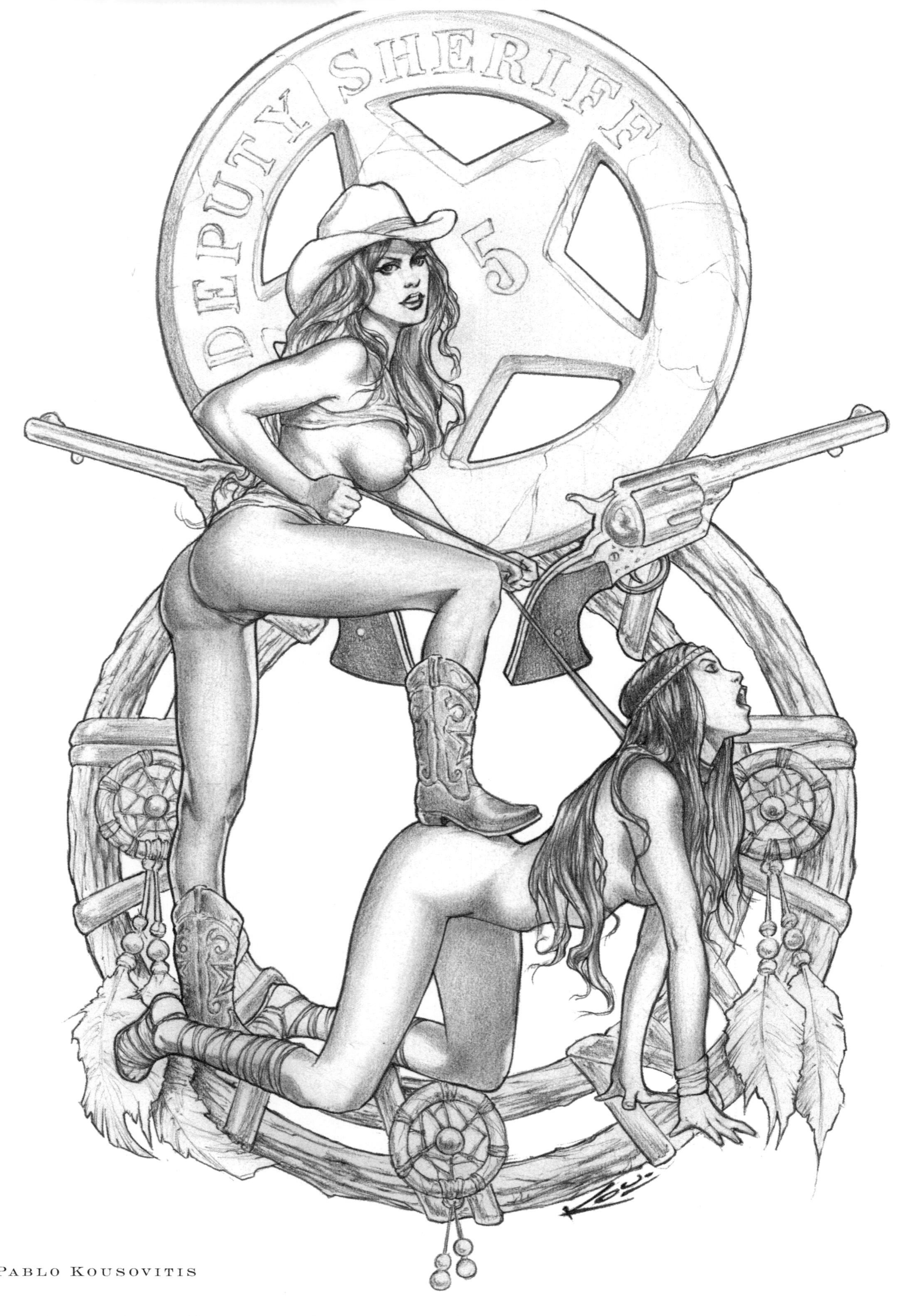

Pablo Kousovitis

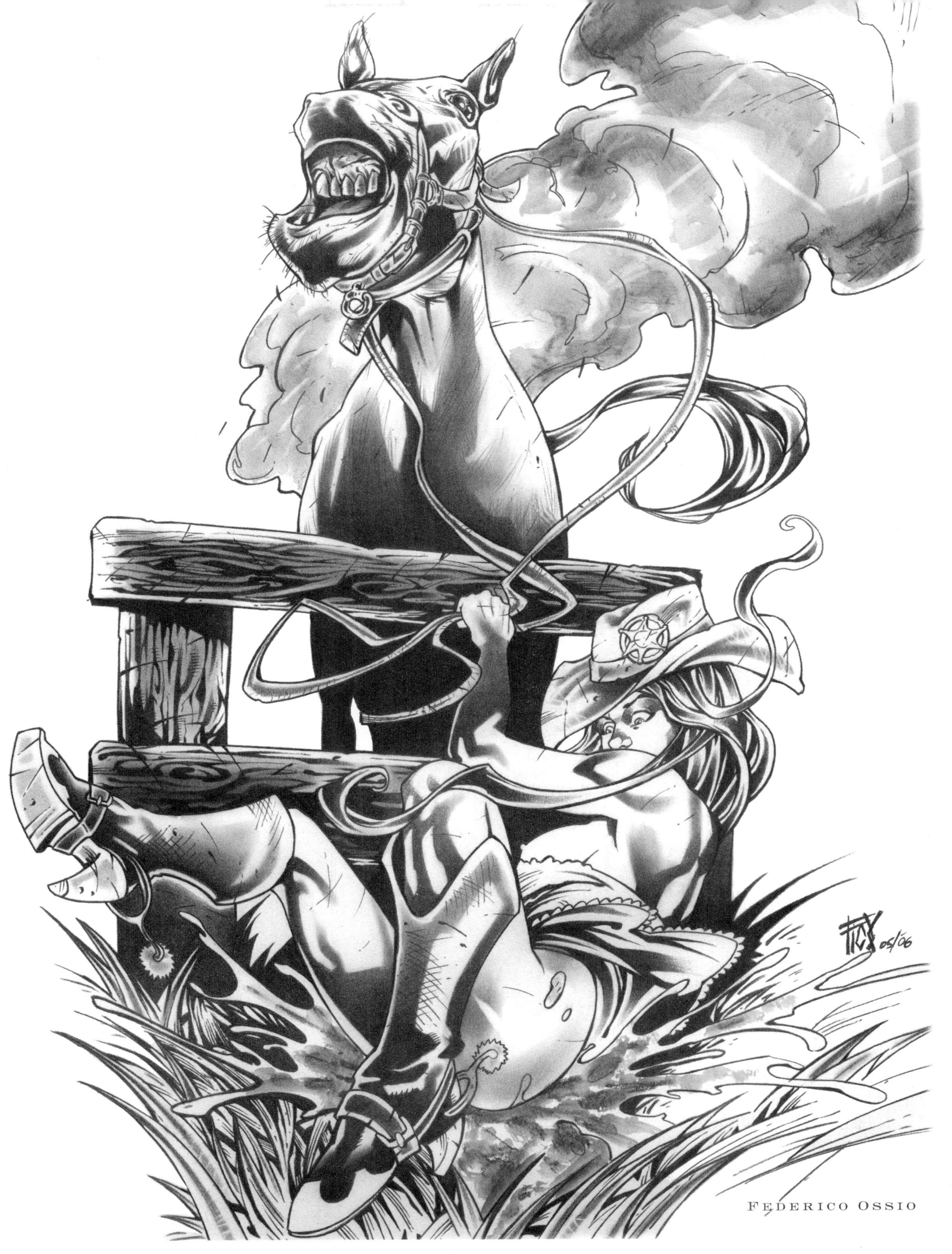

Federico Ossio

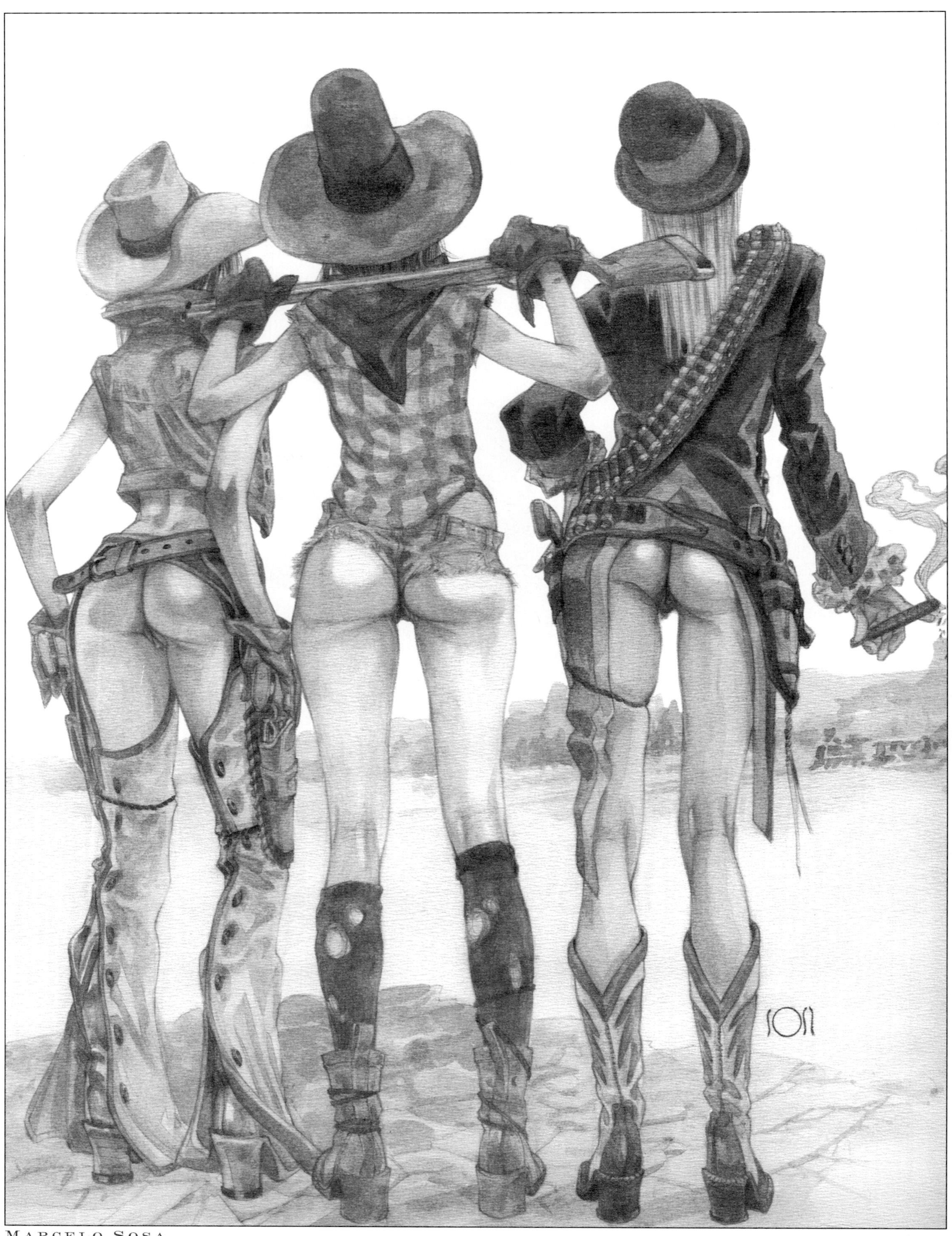

Marcelo Sosa